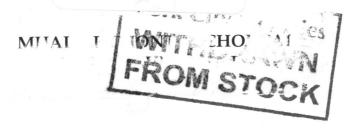

50 Cautionary Tales
for Managers

howtobooks

Please send for a free copy of the latest catalogue:
How To Books
3 Newtec Place, Magdalen Road
Oxford OX4 1RE, United Kingdom
info@howtobooks.co.uk
www.howtobooks.co.uk

50 Cautionary Tales for Managers

AN ENTERTAINING COLLECTION OF ENLIGHTENING
PARABLES FOR MANAGERS

Dr Peter Honey

howtobooks

'I've got this brain that runs on memories.' *Leonard Cohen*

Dedication

For Carol Ann for always being there and ensuring a wonderful work/life balance.

Acknowledgements

To Lesley Bourne and the team for running my business so competently that it gave me time to write this book. Without them, this book would still be unfinished business.

To all the managers I have worked with over many years. Without you, this book could not exist. If you recognise yourself, I can assure you it was someone else!

Published by How To Books Ltd
3 Newtec Place, Magdalen Road
Oxford, OX4 1RE, United Kingdom
Tel: (01865) 793806 Fax: (01865) 248780
email: info@howtobooks.co.uk
http://www.howtobooks.co.uk

Text © Peter Honey 2006
Cartoons © David Mostyn

British Library Cataloguing in Publication Data
A catalogue record for this book is available from the British Library.

Produced for How To Books by Deer Park Productions, Tavistock
Typeset by *specialist* publishing services ltd, Milton Keynes/Montgomery
Cover illustration by David Mostyn
Cover design by Baseline Arts Ltd, Oxford
Printed and bound by Cromwell Press Ltd, Trowbridge, Wiltshire

Note: The material contained in this book is set out in good faith for general guidance and no liability can be accepted for loss or expense incurred as a result of relying in particular circumstances on statements made in the book. The laws and regulations are complex and liable to change, and readers should check the current position with the relevant authorities before making personal arrangements.

Contents

Foreword   vii
Preface   xiii
Introduction   xvii
Part 1: Stories about directors and senior managers   1
1 A manager who wanted solutions, not problems   3
2 A manager who preferred deference to consultation   7
3 A manager who was convinced that his interventions
   made a difference   12
4 A manager who enjoyed victimising graduates   16
5 A manager surrounded by sycophants   21
6 A manager who loved to ask questions   24
7 A manager who liked to keep things simple   30
8 A manager who succumbed to a staff attitude survey   36
9 A manager with a reputation for being calm and unruffled   42
10 A manager who showed his frustration in an unusual way   46
11 A manager who was democratic to a fault   51
12 A manager who was wedded to short-termism   58
13 A manager who lapsed into long silences   64
14 A manager who was desperate to keep in touch   67
15 A manager who couldn't admit he was still learning   72
16 A manager who strove to give a student a really
   interesting week of work experience   78
17 A manager who was hooked on initiatives   85
18 A head teacher who hardly ever put a foot wrong   89
19 A manager with Jekyll and Hyde characteristics   93
20 A manager who was a know-all and went to great lengths
   to win every argument   98
21 A manager who lacked social skills   104
22 A manager who became the victim of unintended consequences 109
23 A manager who failed to walk his talk   114

24 A manager who loved to wander around   119
25 A manager who couldn't resist relying on his
    predecessor's advice   123

Part 2: Stories about middle and junior managers   **129**
26 A manager who insisted words could only be used if
    precise definitions had been agreed   131
27 A manager who sampled 360 degree feedback and
    promptly went into denial   137
28 A manager who thought brainstorming was the answer to
    just about everything   144
29 A manager who couldn't resist tinkering with written reports   149
30 A story about two managers vying for promotion   154
31 A manager who found it convenient to disappear for
    long periods   159
32 A manager who perfected resistance by inertia   163
33 A manager who was reluctant to go home   168
34 An insecure manager clinging on for survival   172
35 A manager with unquenchable enthusiasm   176
36 A manager who was punished for exposing dishonesty   181
37 A manager who thought he was accident prone   186
38 A manager who prided himself on his time management   191
39 A manager who liked to slip away unnoticed   196
40 A manager who oozed clichés   201
41 A manager who encountered fierce resistance   205
42 A manager who stuck to his story   211
43 A manager with a low tolerance for ambiguity   216
44 A manager who got budget dumping down to a fine art   222
45 A manager who recommended ways to improve staff motivation   226
46 A manager who thought he had overslept   232
47 A manager who was too big for his boots   236
48 A manager prone to being caught out   241
49 A manager who reverted to type   245
50 A manager who was prone to tantrums   249
Index   **255**

Foreword

by Geoff Armstrong

Two of the most formative learning experiences of my life came in my first year of working as a graduate trainee in the motor industry. Neither was planned but they shaped my early understanding and approach to management.

The first was when the senior foreman in charge of the swarf house – the scrap reclamation department for the factory – was called into hospital unexpectedly early for a hernia operation. No one suitable was available to take his place, so I was given the wonderful opportunity, working with about twenty much wiser and more experienced blue-collar colleagues, to 'manage' the department for ten weeks.

I made every mistake in the book. The fact that I did not lose the company a fortune was down to my colleagues' perseverance and experience, rather than any contribution I made to the complex, not to say bewildering, array of judgements that needed to be made every day. And the fact that I escaped the sack and was able to learn from my mistakes was down to the counsel and patience of a personnel manager who helped me reflect and refine how I would go about things differently next time.

The second was in that same Coventry factory. Professor Keith Thurley at LSE was doing research into what first and second line managers actually did. Somehow, I became aware of this and persuaded the personnel manager that we should volunteer to take part.

For a week at a time, I shadowed four or five different managers, noting what they did and summarising it in pie charts. Where their job descriptions used words like scheduling, planning, organising, allocating and so on, their actions had a great deal more to do with fixing, compromising, trouble-shooting, progress chasing and being an agony aunt. They were lubricating the management process but were hardly part of it in the sense of determining or directing what went on.

I learned that management is not a universally coherent process and managers don't all do the same things!

Managers are really interesting. They get necessary things done. They multi-task, juggling today's operational priorities, coping with unplanned events and trying to deliver the longer-term strategic intent of the organisations they serve.

Managers are in the front-line of change. It is their job to make sense of the turbulence all around them. Rising customer expectations, fickle markets, disruptive technologies, regulation, competition, globalisation, political, financial and stakeholder pressures are relentless.

Managers have to digest a mass of unclear signals and competing calls for their attention, while optimising the use of resources, maximising performance and projecting a confident future.

Crucially, too, they have to develop, motivate and manage the many people upon whose willing contribution every organisation depends. Employees are not conscripts, conditioned to comply with whatever instructions are handed down to them.

Managers have to ensure that employees have the ability, the motivation and the opportunity to contribute to the level of their potential. They have to craft effective relationships which cause people to want to use their initiative to delight customers, to learn continuously and to apply the fruits of that learning in the interests of the organisation.

Managers make tough choices, often on the basis of imperfect knowledge. The models of systematic analysis, long-term planning and rational decision-making that underpin our management literature are necessary but not sufficient to capture what managers do. Management is also about judgement, experience, intuition when it comes to steering a path through ever-shifting pressures, priorities and accidents that make up reality for organisations across the public, private and voluntary sectors.

Yet we know that most managers are inadequately trained for the job. A tiny minority have formal qualifications or have undertaken serious programmes of learning in management. Doubts are widespread about the value of much of what is on offer in management education. Teaching management as an academic subject, remote from the opportunity to put it into practice, can only be of limited value.

We know from the pioneering work of Alan Mumford, Peter Honey (the author of this book) and others that managers learn best – that is, change their behaviour so that they do things differently – from learning and doing in a practical work situation. The CIPD's (Chartered Institute of Personnel and Development) own research confirms that there has been a shift from training to learning, demanding a different approach to the development of employees. Emphasis in organisations is being shifted from training as a series of top-down interventions to a focus on individual and team learning as on-going activity.

Testing ideas, experimenting, measuring results, reflecting on what works and what doesn't, forming new plans of action, and so on in a continuous and systematic process of learning is how most managers raise their game. Yet, despite the growing recognition of the need to change, most managers still don't have that opportunity. Instead they are thrown in at the deep end and expected to sink or swim, without the support that evidence shows can make a lasting, beneficial impact.

And, finally, managers are human. They suffer from all the insecurity, self-doubt, psychological flaws, blind-spots and less-than-perfect ability to know everything and do it right first time that the rest of us suffer from too.

Peter Honey knows this. His work is sensitive, as well as practical and relevant. In *50 Cautionary Tales for Managers*, he presents real-life people in real-life situations. I recognise and may have met many of the people he describes. I think I'm even there in some of them myself.

With charm and humour, *50 Cautionary Tales for Managers* captures many of the dilemmas of managerial life. With modesty and affection for the managers living the experience, Peter gently suggests how different behaviours might have led to better results.

This book is a good read for managers. It offers short-cuts to learning without having to go through the pain, cost and career risk of learning only from mistakes experienced personally.

Management trainers will find it a rich resource from which to pick hard-edged, realistic case studies to help them in their work.

It will help too, those in public policy grappling with the performance of national economies. We know we have a gap between the need for capable managers and the supply. We have lots of evidence of what makes for effective management and of how to develop it. Joining them together into a strategy which is widely taken up in practice continues to be an elusive target.

Peter's book is a timely reminder of what we know and of how to put it into practice. He doesn't under-estimate the problem. He doesn't preach grand, one-size-fits-all panaceas. And he never forgets that managers are people, with all the needs, wants, flaws and irrationality that people have.

These pen portraits deserve to be read widely, reflected upon and used to stimulate management learning. That will provide a much better return on investment than the alternative, more familiar approaches which have failed us thus far.

Geoff Armstrong
Director General
Chartered Institute of Personnel and Development

Preface

If you are a manager, even if we have never met, I'll guarantee you are in this book! Something you say or do, your management style, a favourite catch-phrase, a mannerism – you'll be here in one or more of these stories.

If you don't recognise yourself, perhaps some of the situations in the stories will be familiar – times when you emerged relatively unscathed or times when you were overwhelmed by events. You will also find stories about managers who are not at all like you; stories about bullies, sexual harassers, arrogant autocrats, chronic ditherers, pedantic meddlers – they are all here.

For over 40 years I have worked with many hundreds of managers of different shapes and sizes, initially because they were my bosses and, since 1969, because they were my clients. I personally knew all the managers who feature in this book. All the stories are based on real-life events with, of course, the occasional bit of artistic licence thrown in for good measure! Naturally, I have changed the names of the managers and I have been careful to avoid identifying any organisations.

I have concluded each story by offering some advice to the central character. I have done this with some trepidation because, in my experience, offering advice, *unless it has been sought*, is usually futile. Even when people ask for advice, it is invariably more acceptable if it emerges through dialogue. The most effective advice, i.e. advice that is a) owned, b) acted upon and c) makes a difference for the better, is best drawn out of the person. Managers are usually perfectly capable of solving their own problems. All they need is a dispassionate sounding board to help them crystallise their ideas.

The advice sections in this book are not therefore a good illustration of the way I would normally approach advising my clients. Despite this, even while masquerading as an agony aunt, I have attempted to adhere to the same guidelines that I would use when facilitating advice, as opposed to simply giving it. These are:

- To converge on one issue, or area for improvement, in order to reduce the risk of overwhelming the manager with numerous options.

- Wherever possible, to maximise the probability of arriving at something practical by focusing on the overt behaviour of the manager, rather than delving deeper into motives, attitudes and feelings.

- To err on the side of recommending actions that the manager will find relatively easy to implement.

- To concentrate on work-based actions rather than recommending courses to go on or other books to read.

Books (especially *management* books) are supposed to be useful; to have some declared purposes. The contents of this book have a number of potential uses.

1. Whether you are a manager, an aspiring manager, or a professional, it has been written to entertain. It could cheer you up as you realise you are not alone – that there are other organisations as crazy as yours! I hope you will chuckle at the exploits of some of the managers you'll find here, and let out a whoop of joy when someone you disapprove of gets the comeuppance they deserve.

2. Since each story has a 'message' and generates some advice, I hope you will find some ideas that are useful to you. In particular, some of the advice sections may provide you with the germ of an idea that you can tailor to fit your particular circumstances.

3. Alternatively, you could ignore the advice sections and use the stories themselves as case studies. They could provide a good,

non-threatening way to stimulate useful discussion about management dilemmas and practices. I once ran a session at a management conference where I told three of these stories and, after each, invited the audience to share their interpretations. Each story generated at least half a dozen different insights. Try it with your team. If you focused on just one story a week, you'd have enough material to keep you going for a year!

4. The book offers you a number of other practical possibilities. If, for example, you have a boss who makes your life a misery, you could mark the relevant passages and send him or her a copy anonymously (mark it 'from a well-wisher'!). Alternatively, if you are brave enough, you could use the book as a way to indulge in some continuing professional development. Simply ask your colleagues or staff to tell you which story (or stories!) are most like you. Then, resisting the temptation to become argumentative, do an honest stock-take of your own managerial ways and decide which to continue and which to curtail.

If all else fails, just relax, go into denial, and enjoy the stories.

All the managers in my stories are men and I have made a conscious decision not to indulge in any gender reversals. There are two reasons for this.

First, without exception, all the quirky managers I have worked with have been male. I have, of course, worked with a few female managers too, but, gratifyingly, they weren't in the least quirky. In fact, they were far too 'normal' to include in this book! This is not a sexist remark. I have also worked with many male managers who weren't sufficiently 'interesting' to qualify for one of my stories. Throughout my career as a management consultant, there have always been far more male managers than female ones. This is hardly surprising. In the decade 1990 to 2000, only 12% of British companies had any female managers at all and, during the same period, only 3% of directors were female. I'm not condoning this state of affairs, simply recognising it as a fact.

Second, I once had an unfortunate experience that taught me that you tinker with genders at your peril. I had prepared six short case studies, each describing a situation that needed to be handled assertively. Participants on the programme I was running were invited to imagine themselves in each situation and to work out how to deal with it assertively. On its first outing a female participant told me in no uncertain terms that my case studies were unacceptable because all the managers were male and all the subordinates were female. I apologised, told her that all the managers in the case studies had in fact been male, and assured her I would make the necessary adjustments.

After the programme I explained the nature of the complaint to my (female) secretary and left her to swap the sexes of some of the managers and subordinates. On the exercise's second outing a female participant said, 'Dr Honey, this is outrageous! All the women are baddies and all the men are goodies.' I apologised and promised to fix the problem.

Together with my secretary, I drew up a grid and spent half a day carefully working out who should be male and who should be female! In the circumstances, I'd rather not face that task with the 50 managers who appear in this book. They really were all male – and I think it best they stay that way.

Peter Honey

Introduction

As I hope the stories in this book will convey, I have a soft spot for managers (well, *most* managers!). I feel sorry for them – especially for middle managers, those much maligned people, uncomfortably sandwiched between those above and those below.

Managers are visible and vulnerable. They are exposed to relentless downward and upward scrutiny, they are the subject of constant speculation and gossip, they make convenient scapegoats and, when their people commit mistakes, they are held accountable (that means blamed!). Not an enviable position to be in.

In my experience, most people didn't actually set out to become managers – certainly not *middle* managers! It was just a horrible accident – the way things worked out. Interestingly, whenever I have asked captains of industry whether they planned to do what they were doing, they have always dropped their voice (as if it was a shameful thing to admit) and told me that they ascribed their glorious careers to a series of coincidences, to being in the right place at the right time, and to sheer opportunism. So much for career planning!

What most managers *really* wanted was to relish being an acclaimed salesperson, scientist, accountant, lawyer or IT expert. Unfortunately they reached a stage in their career where, for various reasons, they had to make the puzzling transition and become a manager. I describe the transition as puzzling because the skills of doing something well yourself and of getting other people to do things well *for you* are so utterly different.

Instead of becoming a world authority in some chosen specialism, managers wrestle daily with a host of open-ended challenges; how to admit that you don't know something without losing face, how to balance short-term tactics with longer-term strategy, how to base sound decisions on inadequate data, how to achieve over-demanding targets whilst nurturing and developing people, how to find and retain talented staff, how to motivate people to do more with less, how to win and retain people's trust, how to keep continuous processes fresh and sustainable, how to be a role model when you don't feel like it, how to achieve a sensible work/life balance, whether to manage or lead or do both ... and so on.

It probably sounds odd to say that I feel sorry for managers. What, those fat cats, those downsizers, those people who are out to exploit the workers? How could you feel sorry for *them*? Well, here are seven good reasons.

1. The perils of delegating and letting go

Every manager, by definition, has a job that is too big to be accomplished singlehanded. It requires other people (variously called subordinates, staff, direct reports or colleagues) to help. Inevitably, therefore, managers must confront the dangerous business of how to delegate, i.e. how to get someone else to do part of their job for them, preferably willingly.

This may sound straightforward, but on closer examination delegation is something of a minefield. For example, the delegating manager has to decide:

- what to delegate;

- how to make it a task with some degree of coherence;

- whom to entrust with part of *their* job;

- whether to risk 'stretch delegation', i.e. where the task is deliberately delegated to someone in order to provide them with a developmental opportunity;

- what authority the person needs in order to carry out the delegated task;

- whether to delegate by sticking to 'whats' and leaving the person to decide 'hows';

- how to delegate so that the person *feels* accountable (even though, in truth, the accountability remains with the manager);

- to what extent to let the person work on the task without supervision;

- how, and when, to follow up – before or after the agreed deadline.

The whole process is fraught with uncertainty. No wonder so many managers are timorous delegators.

2. The perils of losing control

Every organisation has a built-in propensity to fail. Much of what managers do falls into the category of 'maintenance', that is to say, working hard to maintain the *status quo*. An unspoken fear of failure lurks just beneath the surface. Anything that smacks of anarchy or chaos is a threat. The instinctive reaction is to impose authority and tighten control. The overriding belief is that people and processes must be controlled if they are to operate effectively. The maxim is 'people do what's checked, not what you expect'.

Much of the control is, however, illusory. It is impossible for managers, particularly *senior* managers, to know what is going on. The information they are fed is selected and, invariably, laundered. Naturally, managers like to feel they are in touch and that when they tell someone what to do it will be done.

Every day, however, people lower in the hierarchy decide what work is actually done. Managers may have a right to command, but the commanded have a right to decide how far to obey.

Of course, managers are under pressure to relinquish some of their control and empower people to 'see what's important and do it'. But in my experience, most managers are wary of letting go. It seems to them little short of suicidal. They are even wary of more participation (a fraction of what is involved in letting go!). It seems messy and time-consuming and people might make the wrong decision.

So, beleaguered managers, bombarded with messages about the need to encourage their people to take responsibility, are racked with doubt about the wisdom of letting go. It reminds me of the old navy saying:

> *Now hear this,*
> *Now hear this.*
> *This is the captain speaking,*
> *This is the captain speaking.*
> *That is all,*
> *That is all.* [1]

3. The perils of developing people

Managers know they are supposed to develop their people's talents by providing them with ample opportunities to acquire new knowledge and skills. They even understand the benefits of doing so; competent staff are more dependable and make fewer mistakes.

However, it is one thing to understand this intellectually and quite another to make it a daily priority. The gap between managers' knowing and doing is usually at its widest when it comes to people management.

Most managers are highly embarrassed when it comes to giving people honest feedback – either praise or criticism – or of conducting appraisals, or of having any sort of constructive discussion about someone's performance. They don't know what to say and worry that the conversation could get out of hand or that someone could get upset. It is far easier to avoid such vague, emotive topics and stick to safe things like the latest share price or even the weather!

Managers have a perfect excuse to fudge developing people. They know that sooner or later their best people will be poached or promoted. Better, therefore, not to bring them on in the first place or, if they are already competent, to hide them.

4. The perils of keeping up the pretence

Managers are human. They have off-days, days when they don't feel like keeping up the pretence that they are omnipotent. Yet they are expected to appear keen and enthusiastic, to exude a 'can do' attitude, to 'walk the talk', to 'do the vision thing'.

I have always been critical of those books that suggest managers need to be 'super' or 'great' or 'incredible'. I find the calls to walk on water unrealistic and depressing, and, should such propaganda be believed, it runs the risk of making managers feel even more inadequate. Good managers don't need to be miracle workers. They just need to be honest and resilient enough to keep going in the face of difficulties and setbacks.

Managers, however, are understandably loath to drop the facade. Imagine a manager saying 'I don't know' or 'I don't think we have the slightest chance of achieving this target' or, even more unlikely, 'I was wrong and I'm pleased to announce a U-turn.' Imagine a manager calling his or her staff together and saying, 'I am suffering from low self-esteem and paranoia and I can't keep up the pretence any longer. From now on I'm going to be me.'

Sadly, managers are role models whether they like it or not. Their staff take an unhealthy interest in all that they say and do. I have known entire organisations come to a halt as rumours spread about the CEO's latest crazy idea, the next hare-brained initiative or a boardroom coup.

5. The perils of loneliness

Managers have few people they can trust with confidences. The climate in most organisations encourages protecting your back and fighting off predators. Few managers feel genuinely secure.

Quite understandably, therefore, managers expend much time and energy ensuring that they keep safe and blame-free. Who can you turn to for advice and guidance – perhaps even for some honest feedback? Increasingly the answer is to an external coach or mentor, someone who has no axe to grind, someone who doesn't covet your job. To admit inadequacies and secret worries to a colleague, or to your boss, would be considered naïve and 'career limiting'.

I have known many managers who appeared to be robust and self-sufficient, but who, in reality, were feeling exposed and frightened. Once they came to trust me, out would pour stories of woe – stories of victimisation, stories of impossible demands and expectations, stories of confusion and ambiguity and, of course, stories of inadequate subordinates.

Feeling vulnerable saps energy and hampers creativity and bold decision-making. It makes it likely that managers will indulge in 'analysis to paralysis' and hide behind committee decisions. It also erodes self-confidence and drives managers to increase their efforts to pretend they know what they are doing.

6. The perils of not knowing whether to lead or manage

Despite all the current emphasis on leadership, few managers are clear whether managing *is* leading or whether there is a significant difference between the two. I'm not at all surprised. I am the first to admit (easy for me, I'm not a manager!) that I'm not at all sure what leadership is and where managing stops and leading begins.

I have studied those lists that purport to distinguish between managing and leading. You know the sort of thing:

Managers	Leaders
Administer	Innovate
Keep their eye on the bottom line	Keep their eye on the horizon
Ask 'how' and 'when'	Ask 'what' and 'why'
Do things right	Do the right things
Make incremental changes	Make transformational changes
Delegate	Empower

But I always find the overlaps greater than the differences, with the boundaries so fuzzy as to be indistinguishable. Surely managers need to lead and leaders need to manage? Doesn't everyone need to be ambidextrous?

Then we have those lists of characteristics that researchers claim successful leaders display. Warren Bennis, for example, the well-known writer on leadership, lists five characteristics that his studies of 150 'outstanding' leaders revealed. They all displayed:

1. A strong sense of purpose, a passion, a conviction, a sense of wanting to do something important to make a difference.

2. The capacity to develop and sustain deep and trusting relationships.

3. Positive illusions of reality allowing them to be the 'purveyors of hope'.

4. A balance in their lives between work, power, and family or outside activities.

5. A bias towards action and risk taking. [2]

For me, lists like this raise more questions than they answer. Might these five characteristics be coincidental to the success of these leaders? Are these *the* critical characteristics or just the ones Warren Bennis happens to favour? What about all those other characteristics that other researchers list? How many leaders, despite having these five characteristics, failed – overwhelmed by circumstances beyond their control? Do you have to be a paragon of virtue before you can be a good leader?

Finally, we have those lists that read like recipes for successful leadership – especially in times of change (and that is *all the time*!):

1. Set the vision.

2. Communicate it.

3. Secure agreement from key stakeholders.

4. Identify the values and behaviours that are consistent with the vision.

5. Incorporate them into the performance management systems.

And so on. I find recipes like this arrogant because they assume that this is The Answer regardless of the situation. It is yet another version of 'one size fits all'. They are too generic, too tidy, too linear. Try as we might, the complexities of managing and leading cannot be reduced to mere lists.

7. The perils of expecting to be provided with The Answer

Managers, as they wrestle with numerous open-ended problems, are eminently suggestible. They harbour the illusion that someone, somewhere has The Answer. It is psychologically more comforting to treat open-ended problems (i.e. problems where there are numerous possible solutions) as if they were close-ended (i.e. problems where there is a single right answer if only you could locate it). In their heart of hearts, managers know perfectly well that right answers are few and far between.

Managers are under constant bombardment from persuasive gurus peddling the latest management fad(s). Band wagons come and go: management by objectives, participatory management, matrix management, zero-based budgeting, management by walking around, process re-engineering, quality circles, self-managed teams.

An understandable yearning for answers makes managers particularly susceptible to rhetoric about the need to stay nimble in the face of relentless change. They are so fearful of losing competitive advantage that they dare not ignore a fad in case, against all expectations, it proves to be a winner (and, perish the thought, a competitor successfully exploits it). Small wonder that managers are so suggestible.

So, despite a catalogue of disappointments, somehow the appetite for new answers remains. The proliferation of management fads from the supply side is hardly surprising – gurus need to sell their latest book. Meanwhile, poor managers announce another initiative and allow themselves to believe that this one really will make a difference.

In conclusion

On balance, therefore, I sympathise (perhaps a better word would be empathise) with managers. Most managers I have worked with (alas, not all) have had their hearts in the right place and were trying, under difficult circumstances, to do their best. It is just that so many of them exhibited the sort of flawed behaviour patterns that Dotlich and Cairo describe in their book *Why CEOs Fail*.

Aloofness – managers who are disengaged and disconnected.
Arrogance – managers who are convinced they are right and everyone else is wrong.
Eagerness to please – managers who court popularity above all else.
Eccentricity – managers who revel in being different just for the hell of it.
Excessive caution – managers who are afraid to make decisions.
Habitual distrust – managers who are convinced people can't be trusted to do a good job

Melodrama – managers who have to be the centre of attention.
Mischievousness – managers who believe rules are made to be broken.
Passive resistance – managers whose silence is interpreted as agreement.
Perfectionism – managers who concentrate on getting the little things right while the big things go wrong.
Volatility – managers who have sudden mood swings.[3]

Recently, when invited to address management conferences, I have concluded my remarks by getting the audience to join me in a rendering of *The Line Manager's Lament*. I sing (well, chant!) the verses and the audience sings the chorus. Afterwards, managers always tell me how true it was and ask me for a copy of the words (so that they, in turn, can sing it with their colleagues?).

Here are the words so that you too can sing along.

Oh, I can't ensure my staff understand the company's aims and vision and show how their work fits into a wider context.
Chorus: *Because I'm too busy.*

Oh, I can't ensure my staff know what is expected of them and where to go for direction, support and information.
Because I'm too busy.

Oh, I can't help my staff plan and prioritise their work to meet objectives in the time available.
Because I'm too busy.

Oh, I can't spend time getting to know and understand the needs of my staff or to plan their growth and development.
Because I'm too busy.

Oh, I can't lead by example and inspire and communicate

effectively with my staff.
Because I'm too busy.

Oh, I can't delegate responsibility and authority to my staff and balance controls with freedoms.
Because I'm too busy.

Oh, I can't encourage my staff to operate as a team with a shared purpose and to co-operate in such a way that they achieve synergy.
Because I'm too busy.

Oh, I can't give my staff constructive feedback and recognition for good performance.
Because I'm too busy.

Oh, I can't provide on-the-job coaching for my staff and create a supportive learning environment.
Because I'm too busy.

In fact, there is no way I can manage my people effectively. They just have to do the best they can without me and I will feel better by calling it empowerment.
Because I'm too busy.

---

[1] Taken from Chapter 2 of *The Empowered Manager* by Peter Block, published by Jossey-Bass, 1991.

[2] Adapted from *Managing People is like Herding Cats* by Warren Bennis, published by Kogan Page, 1998.

[3] From *Why CEOs Fail* by David L Dotlich and Peter C Cairo, published by Jossey-Bass, 2003.

Part 1:
Stories about directors and senior managers

See Chapter 5

1

A manager who wanted solutions, not problems

Ian enjoyed a reputation as a trouble-shooter *par excellence*. He had been recruited by head-hunters on behalf of a firm that had grown rapidly through a series of acquisitions and ill-advised mergers. Ian's brief, as the newly appointed CEO, was to sort out the mess and return the organisation to profitability – fast. The board was impatient for results and so was Ian, who stood to gain a handsome performance-related bonus.

Ian set to work with his usual vigour. There were many outward signs that he was bubbling with energy; for example, he jiggled his legs and frequently leapt up and paced around in meetings (no deep vain thrombosis for him!) and he was forever straightening pictures. He also had the strange habit of striding along corridors clicking his fingers loudly.

His first action was to make it clear to his direct reports that he didn't want them to bother him with problems, only with solutions. In fact, he found it hard to accept that problems existed at all. Many years ago he had been impressed by a management guru who had argued passionately (the way they do) that problems were best regarded as challenges. So, whereas you would normally think of a solution as the answer to a thing called a problem, Ian thought of solutions as the answers to challenges!

Ian's direct reports, though, found it hard to adjust to this new

3

approach. The previous CEO had *loved* problems (so much so that, by the time he left under a cloud, he had succeeded in creating enough to bring the company to the brink of ruin). In fact, he had positively welcomed anyone who came to him with a problem and insisted it was added it to a long list of problems he captured on a white board in his office (he had curtains fitted that rendered the problems invisible when he received outside visitors!).

Anyway, with this immediate past history, you can perhaps understand why Ian's direct reports had some difficulty adapting to Ian's 'solutions only' approach. Whenever they lapsed into problem-stating behaviour, Ian would become extremely agitated and banish them until they could think of some solutions. This they found hard to do, convinced in their hearts that problems not only existed, but that the ones they were grappling with were insoluble!

So, increasingly, they kept clear of Ian, knowing that if they dared to broach problems (particularly insoluble ones!) they would incur his wrath.

It didn't take Ian long to realise that his direct reports were failing to deliver results and he became exceedingly frustrated about the lack of progress. Naturally he remonstrated with them, explaining over and over again the importance of proposing solutions. 'That's what you're paid for – to spot challenges and produce SOLUTIONS!' But it was to no avail. The more Ian fretted, the more his direct reports took fright and suffered from solution paralysis.

Eventually, Ian called a crisis meeting and demanded an explanation. 'What's the problem?' he shrieked, slamming his fist down on the table. But his direct reports, flabbergasted to hear Ian using the P word, couldn't bring themselves to tell him that the problem was him!

4

Advice to Ian

I know you are under pressure to get results, but if your objective is to get positive solutions from your direct reports, then you are going about it the wrong way. Face up to the fact that your current strategy isn't working and that the more you remonstrate and thump the table, the more your directors will clam up. Your insistence on solutions, not problems, has your directors running scared. Unfortunately your predecessor welcomed problems, and it will take some time to wean the people you have inherited off them.

What should you do?

First, lift your absurd ban on problems and acknowledge that they are a useful starting point, if you like, a stepping stone towards a solution. Think of a problem as a gap; an expression of the difference between what you've got and what you want. Identifying gaps is definitely to be encouraged.

You will need to coach your directors to bring about a change in their behaviour. Here is a brief description of how you could do this:

- When someone points out a problem, ask them what they want in place of what they've got. This will help them to describe the other side (the more positive side) of the gap.

- Second, ease them into thinking of possible solutions, i.e. ways to close the gap. Invite them to come up with options and give them time to ponder this, rather than expecting instant solutions.

- Third, when they offer some options, ask them for their favourite three and for their reasons why. Tease out the pros and cons of each.

- Finally, delegate the task of implementing the agreed solution and decide what help you will offer and what follow-up is necessary. The extent of the help you offer, and frequency of progress reviews, will clearly depend on the magnitude of the task.

Adopt this approach, and I'll guarantee your directors will learn to take responsibility for solving problems. You may even reach a stage where they solve a problem and tell you about it *after* it has been fixed!

2
A manager who preferred deference to consultation

Digby was the CEO of a merchant bank. He had been with the bank since leaving school, starting as a clerk and working his way up to the top job. Now silver-haired and approaching retirement, he occupied an office in the City with a fine view of a couple of Wren churches and, beyond, a glimpse of the Thames. His office was lush and spacious and on the walls hung oil portraits of some of his predecessors (all looking suitably stern).

The bank suffered from institutionalised deference. In its long and glorious history it had moved grudgingly from a command-and-control culture to being slightly (ever so slightly!) more consultative. Traditional managers such as Digby, however, found anything that smacked of democracy very puzzling and inconvenient. It was so much simpler to tell everyone what to do and demand unquestioning obedience. Asking for opinions invariably meant tapping into a host of irreconcilable differences and, in the end, having to say, 'Forget I asked. We'll do it my way.'

With the bank's long history of built-in deference, staff operated with two switches. One was marked 'bow, scrape and agree with everything', and the other was marked 'rant, rave and complain'. Needless to say, the former switch was thrown whenever senior managers were present and the latter switch as soon as their backs were turned.

Digby allowed himself to be persuaded to run a series of workshops for the managers in the bank on the subject of change. This was because the bank were overhauling their antiquated job grading system and the process had thrown up a number of serious anomalies. A two-day workshop was devised where managers would work in small teams, identifying changes they thought necessary and putting forward recommendations for action. Digby agreed to 'bless' each workshop by saying a few words at the start about the need for change and to return for the final plenary session to listen to the recommendations.

The workshop ran nine times in order to accommodate all the managers it was designed to reach. The participants on each workshop differed, but the pattern of events was uncannily similar. Digby would sweep in at the start and read a short speech from a lectern. There were a couple of vaguely light-hearted remarks that always evoked polite laughter. He didn't invite any questions (far too consultative for Digby) but always finished by saying how much he looked forward to returning the next day to hear the recommendations.

As soon as Digby left the room, all hell broke loose as the managers spluttered their wrath at his condescending manner. The 'rant and rave' switches had been thrown.

Once the managers had calmed down, they settled to the task of prioritising the many changes they thought necessary to improve the bank's performance, to brainstorming ways forward and to preparing persuasive presentations. Throughout, ranting and raving was much in evidence as the managers steeled themselves for Digby's return.

Time for the final plenary came eventually and Digby would arrive with a couple of other directors in tow. Switches were immediately turned to 'bow and scrape'. The fighting talk of the last two days simply evaporated without trace. Each presentation consisted of half-hearted insinuations and meaningless platitudes. After hearing all the presentations, Digby would stand, politely thank everyone for their contribution and then calmly dismantle each idea by explaining why it wouldn't work. The participants, of course, sat there nodding deferentially whilst seething inside.

Everyone thought the workshops were a charade. Digby, however, was *very* pleased with them. For him they were proof that consultation didn't work!

Advice to Digby

I know you find democracy messy and inconvenient but I wonder if you would be prepared to try a small experiment? I'm gambling that if you carry this out to the letter, you will find that your staff have some ideas that are worthy of your attention.

Select any department in the bank and ask the staff, anonymously, to rate the following five statements on a scale of 1–10, where '1' signifies 'to no extent' and '10' signifies 'to a very great extent'.

1. To what extent do you feel able to express your ideas and make suggestions for improvement?

2. To what extent do you feel able to say what you really think without having to worry about whether it will meet with approval?

3. To what extent are you free from coercion/pressure to conform and acquiesce?

4. To what extent do you feel able to challenge and confront authority figures?

5. To what extent are you free from the domination and control of more senior people?

Analyse the results and find which statement gets the lowest score.

Form a project team and give them the task of coming up with ideas about what needs to be done to increase the score on the chosen item. So, for example, if item 1 got the lowest score, you'd ask the project team:

'How could we create a climate where people felt able to express their ideas/make suggestions for improvement?' If item 4 got the lowest score, you'd ask 'How could we create a climate where people felt free to challenge and confront those in authority?'

Arrange for the project team to make its recommendations to you in person. When they are presenting their ideas, concentrate on finding at least three things you like. Make it a rule that you will tell them the three things you like *before* you allow yourself to state a concern. Limit yourself to only one concern so that what you say has a ratio of three positives to one negative. Make sure the concern (singular) is posed as a question to the team, 'How could we persuade managers to suspend judgement?' This makes it more likely that the concern will generate more ideas rather than killing things off.

Watch the effect this has on the project team's behaviour. They may be incredulous (because they will be expecting their ideas to be dismissed) but they will also look pleased and may even be brave enough to say more in support of their ideas.

Thank the team and say you will give their ideas careful consideration. Give them a date by when you will come back to them with your decision.

If you discipline yourself a) to ask people for their ideas and b) to say three things you like before stating a concern, you will gradually find people will open up and be more forthcoming. You will also find that the quality of the ideas will increase so that more things are acceptable your eyes and you will want to back them. You can comfort yourself that this is only consultation, not full-blown collaboration, and you are still the final arbiter of what gets implemented.

3

A manager who was convinced that his interventions made a difference

Rod was the general manager of a car assembly plant. An engineer by training, he had spent his entire career in the car manufacturing business and knew the industry inside out. Eventually, just by dint of keeping out of trouble and having worked at the plant longer than any other members of the management team, Rod was promoted to the top job. But he knew he was operating at the margins of his competence. He shut himself away for long periods in the rarefied atmosphere of his panelled office, well away from the hustle and bustle of the assembly line. Abdication (Rod thought of it as delegation) was his way of coping with a threatening world – except in a crisis where, he would become very agitated and rant and rave indiscriminately.

The assembly plant housed four different assembly lines. The newest line used the latest robot technology with very few human beings in attendance. The oldest, by contrast, were very labour-intensive and, despite regular preventive maintenance, sometimes broke down. A stoppage was serious because it jeopardised the production targets that dominated the culture of the plant. The targets for each shift, together with feedback about 'actuals against targets', were clearly displayed for all to see.

On the rare occasions when a line ground to a halt, a maintenance team, always in attendance (they spent most of their time playing cards), swung into action. Their task was to diagnose the cause of the breakdown and get the line running again as fast as possible. The average time for a line to be stationary was 15 minutes.

When a line stopped, a loud siren would sound. It was as if the all-important production targets were letting out a cry of distress. Immediately supervisors and managers in the vicinity would gather round, looking anxious and worried, and watch the maintenance team at work. After about five minutes, even more senior managers would arrive, huffing and puffing. They would also stand around, muttering and looking at their watches. After about 12 minutes, Rod himself would arrive (his office, remember, was some distance away) and proceed to shout abuse at everybody. After approximately 15 minutes, the maintenance team would have done enough to start the line moving again.

This sequence of events occurred four or five times a year and Rod was convinced that it was only when he intervened personally that the problem was fixed. In his view, all the supervisors and managers who arrived at the scene before him were inept since they had failed to get the line moving again before he arrived and saved the day.

Once, the line broke down when Rod was on holiday so he wasn't there to rant and rave. The line still took approximately 15 minutes to fix, but Rod dismissed this inconvenient fact as sheer coincidence. The possibility that his interventions were irrelevant was, quite simply, too terrible for him contemplate.

Advice to Rod

Clearly, the whole idea of intervening is to do so in such a way that it makes a difference *for the better*. It is the *effect* of an intervention that counts. There are only three possible outcomes. An intervention:

- Makes things better.

- Makes no difference.

- Makes things worse.

The most charitable interpretation is that your interventions fall into the middle category. If so, you are wasting your breath and you'd be better off staying in your office. It is quite possible, however, that shouting abuse at everybody has a detrimental effect. Perhaps the maintenance team would work more effectively without all the unwelcome attention from the sidelines. Almost certainly, the supervisors and managers who are the butt of your verbal onslaughts, go away feeling put upon and undervalued.

In fact, the whole situation is absurd and you should take the following steps to break the mould.

1. Assume that it is inevitable that the line will break down from time to time and that, when it does, it will usually take 15 minutes to get it going again.

2. Also, assume that the members of the maintenance team are keen and competent (if they are not, you'd better establish what needs to be done to bring them up to scratch).

3. Tell all your supervisors and managers that you trust the maintenance team to do their stuff and that, when the line

stops, you no longer want to see managers congregating at the scene.

4. The next time the line stops, stay in your office until it has started again. Then, and only then, pay a visit to the maintenance team with the express purpose of congratulating them on a job well done. You might also enquire, casually, whether they had an audience!

5. If you are so twitchy that you find it impossible to stay put in your office, go outside for a brisk 15 minute walk, and then pay a visit to the maintenance team to express your pleasure.

6. A few days after the breakdown, hold a calm, analytical review meeting with the manager of the maintenance team to see what can be learned from the incident and whether there are preventative maintenance implications.

7. Finally, send everyone a note thanking them for their co-operation and congratulating them on their admirable self-control in testing circumstances.

If you follow these steps, you will succeed in converting a useless intervention into a useful, supportive one. That is exactly what managers are supposed to do; make helpful interventions that make a difference for the better.

4

A manager who enjoyed victimising graduates

Bob was the managing director of a publishing company. Small in stature (he stood 5 feet 4 inches tall) he attempted to compensate by being a larger than life character. He was a self-made man with a chip on his shoulder about anyone better educated than him. He had failed the 11-plus and gone to a secondary modern school that he had left at the earliest opportunity, aged 16. He claimed to have been taught only woodwork and knitting for four years and to have read *Kidnapped* by Robert Louis Stevenson in class half a dozen times. This was because he had a Scottish teacher who was crazy about the book and, as it happens, also about the woodwork teacher! Bob took great pride in telling people about concealed dovetail joints and in his office he even had a coffee table he had made whilst at school.

He regarded anyone with a university education as fair game – targets for a relentless barrage of put-downs. This meant that most of his staff were in the firing line. He would take every opportunity to belittle them and, if opportunities didn't arise in the normal course of events, he created them.

One of his favourite techniques was to inflict a general knowledge quiz on his unsuspecting staff. Bob compiled the quiz so he knew all the answers (one of his little jokes was to announce the quiz by saying 'Here's one I prepared earlier'). The contents of the quiz were deliberately obscure. If someone dared to answer correctly, Bob would go berserk and accuse them of being geeks and know-alls. People quickly learned not to produce a correct answer – or even to risk an inspired guess in case it turned out to be accurate.

Another device he used to 'prove' he was smarter than everyone else, was to delegate tasks but to withhold vital information. This virtually guaranteed that the delegatee would fail, and made it easy for Bob to ridicule the inadequacies of their work.

Bob was even more vindictive towards female graduates. Plump girls with big bosoms were irresistible targets. He'd single them out one by one, summon them to his office, and tell them they were disgustingly fat and demand to know what they were going to do about it. He'd only let them go once he had reduced them to tears. Bare midriffs, regardless of whether you were fat or not, were very dangerous items to have on show if Bob was around. He'd look pointedly at the offending navel and shout, 'I know you were born. I don't need to see the evidence!'

He enjoyed telling sexist jokes at inappropriate times in inappropriate company. One of his favourites was about a well-endowed woman who went to her doctor worried about a lump in her breast. The doctor asked her to strip to the waist so that he could examine her breasts. When she emerged from behind the screen he saw that she had large breasts and asked if he might weigh them. The woman was surprised, but assumed it must be a routine part of the check-up. To her astonishment, he cupped each breast in his hands, joggled them up and down, flung his head back and shouted 'whey!'.

All in all, Bob was a little shit. As you might guess, staff turnover was high – not just females but males too. This didn't seem to trouble Bob in the least. In fact, he took it as a sign of his effectiveness, 'Good riddance!' he'd say, followed by one of his favourite mantras, 'If you can't stand the heat, get out of the kitchen.'

One day Bob's secretary (a thin woman who wisely never showed her midriff) found Bob in his office in tears. Never having seen him in such a state before, indeed never having believed he was capable of tears, she assumed he had received news of some catastrophe.

'What's wrong?' she asked, fearing the worst.

'My wife has just phoned', sobbed Bob. 'She says the dog has taken a turn for the worse and the vet says it would be best to put it out of its misery.'

It seems that even bullies have soft spots.

Advice to Bob

Your behaviour towards graduates is, quite simply, unacceptable. You are abusing your power and having a detrimental effect on staff morale and turnover. In your heart of hearts, you must know this.

Presumably, you single out graduates for harassment because you still deeply resent the fact that you didn't have the opportunity to go to university yourself. You could, of course, put this right by enrolling on an Open University programme that would eventually result in the award of an honours degree. Alternatively, if that seems too long a haul, why not enrol yourself on some prestigious business school course? You have plenty of choice – the London Business School, Ashridge, even Harvard – somewhere like that. This would give you a worthwhile qualification more quickly and you'd have the pleasure of mixing with people of similar status/seniority to yourself.

If you reject the idea of gaining a qualification, then you'll have to find some other way to get to feel better about yourself without having to taunt your graduates. How about setting yourself a challenge, running in a marathon for example or immersing yourself in a worthy cause? With your management expertise you could quickly become chairman of your local Citizen's Advice Bureau or the Health Authority for your area. Voluntary organisations are always looking for people with business experience. There are plenty of opportunities to make a contribution in your local community and 'give something back'. Why, you could even finish up with a medal!

The key, I'm sure, is to tackle something with high visibility that you can justifiably feel proud of. By proving yourself in the areas where, at present, you feel inadequate, you would soon feel on a par with all those bright young graduates you keep victimising.

There are massive benefits for you (the most important benefit as far as you are concerned!), for your organisation as a whole and for your staff.

5

A manager surrounded by sycophants

Robin was an entrepreneur with all the usual characteristics; infectious curiosity, enthusiasm and the ability to produce a vast number of unconventional ideas. He had the habit of leaning back in his chair, gazing up at the ceiling with both hands clasped behind his head and releasing a steady stream of lateral thoughts. Edward de Bono would have been proud of him!

Inevitably, many of his ideas were entirely speculative but members of his management team developed an alarming tendency to hang on to his every word and assume he was serious (that the ideas were vertical, not lateral). This meant that time and energy were wasted working on ideas that Robin never intended to be taken seriously (and, indeed, had invariably forgotten!).

Robin became increasingly disappointed with his colleagues. He complained that he was surrounded by sycophants who never challenged any of his suggestions. He became so desperate that he hired a consultant as a sort of mentor with a specific brief to disagree with him! Whilst sympathising with his plight, the consultant had misgivings about this role but agreed to try it for an experimental three-month period.

There was, however, a serious problem. As the consultant sat in on Robin's board meetings, he would listen to him spinning off his ideas

and think to himself, 'He is absolutely right' and 'What a brilliant notion' and 'Wow, this man is amazing'. In short, the consultant would succumb to sycophantic thoughts that were the direct opposite of the challenging behaviour that Robin expected of him. Invariably, it was while the consultant was in the grip of positive feelings and deep admiration that Robin would look pointedly at the consultant and invite his opinion. That was the cue for the consultant to put forward counter-arguments and objections.

Now, it is very difficult to dispute with someone when you are in wholehearted agreement with them. The consultant did his best, of course, but he knew that his faked arguments were essentially feeble and half-hearted. They were easily demolished, not only by Robin, but also by members of his team, who clearly relished the extra opportunities to demonstrate their support for Robin.

After the three-month trial, Robin and the consultant met for a review. The consultant had come to the conclusion that he should admit defeat and jump before he was pushed. At the very start of the meeting, therefore, he said that he didn't think the arrangement was working and that it should be brought to an end. To his astonishment, Robin said he was delighted with the consultant's help and wished to continue with the relationship. However, the consultant dug his heels in and refused. Eventually, they agreed to differ and go their separate ways.

That was the first and only time that the consultant succeeded in disagreeing with Robin and winning his point!

Advice to Robin

You are going to have to find a way to send clearer signals to your staff. At present they are failing to discriminate between ideas that need to be developed and acted upon and ideas that are purely speculative and 'off-the-top-of-the-head'. This wastes time and resources and clearly causes you irritation.

All this is avoidable if you used a simple category system. When you throw out ideas (don't stop doing this – it is clearly one of your strengths), code them as follows:

1. Develop this idea and implement it.

2. Develop this idea, but run it past me *before* you implement anything.

3. I'd like you to consider whether this idea has any mileage – but be sure to discuss it with me before you make any plans to implement it.

4. This idea is half-baked, I need to give it more consideration before you do anything.

5. Forget I ever said this!

Just five categories will do the trick. Eventually, when this system is ingrained, if you forget to categorise an idea, your direct reports will seek clarification: 'Is that a 1 or a 2?' 'I take it that is a 5?.'

They might even reach a stage where mutual understanding is so good that they don't have to ask at all. Heaven!

6

A manager who loved to ask questions

Tom was the research and development director in an international pharmaceutical company. He had a team of highly qualified researchers (mostly PhDs) working on a variety of long-term research projects and drug trials. Time spans for these activities often stretched 10 or more years into the future and the company invested large sums of money speculating that at least some of the projects would come to fruition.

Tom's office was on the top floor of a new building that contained a number of state-of-the-art laboratories. The atmosphere throughout was similar to a red-brick university (apart from the high security fence that surrounded the 'campus' to deter animal rights protesters). On the ground floor, to the left of the reception area, was a well-stocked reference library with all the latest scientific journals. Each floor of the building contained spacious meeting places where people could linger over a slice of carrot cake and a cup of coffee. There was a gymnasium full of treadmills and exercise bikes. The gardens featured many benches either side of landscaped brick paths winding through beds of shrubs and lily ponds.

Tom himself was an academic with an international reputation. He had published many learned papers and often read them (literally!) to delegates at conferences in remote parts of the world. Tom's office commanded fine views across rolling countryside and Tom would often stand gazing out of the plate glass window, deep in thought about some obscure chemical formula.

Tom's style was entirely in keeping with these enlightened surroundings. He was gentle and reflective, never aggressive or forceful. He was happy to mull over ideas, indefinitely if left to his own devices, to see what might, just might, emerge. He often reminded people that all ideas had to pass through a stage where they could easily be criticised. He treated ideas in rather the same way that a nurseryman would nurture tender shoots – with much loving care. On his wall was a framed version (in superb calligraphy with many flourishes) of the well-known prayer:

> *Grant me the serenity to accept the things I cannot change, the courage to change the things I can and the wisdom to know the difference.*

It is fair to say that Tom was more at peace with the things he couldn't change than with the things he could.

Tom was also a great believer in the power of questions. He saw them as a conduit for ideas and totally subscribed to the view, first voiced, he acknowledged, by the American economist Thorstein Bunde Veblen in 1919, that the outcome of any serious research was to make two questions grow where only one grew before.

Such was Tom's dedication to the asking of questions that he used various techniques for generating them. For example, in meetings if there was an imbalance between statements and questions (the usual state of affairs), the 'Three questions rule' would be artificially imposed on the proceedings. This required each participant to pose three questions before being allowed to utter one statement. A ratio of three questions to one statement worked wonders! Other methods included being confined to asking open-ended questions, posing problems as questions – 'In how many ways can we …?' – and playing 'what if?' games with countless scenarios.

Unhappily, Tom's prowess at asking, and eliciting, insightful questions was not matched by his ability to produce answers. He was fond of saying (a touch defensively), 'Questions that can be answered aren't worth asking.' As a scientist, no doubt his addiction to intriguing, open-ended questions stood him in good stead, but as a manager (some would say leader) his inability to produce answers caused endless frustration. Tom would even dither if you asked him simple questions such as whether he'd prefer tea or coffee, or whether he'd like the window open or closed. When it came to decisions about whether to hire or fire someone, or whether to reallocate funds from one budget to another, or whether to update the job grading system, he would procrastinate with a capital P.

One day, in a management meeting with his team during which Tom had evaded and equivocated over every question put to him, an incredulous newcomer asked Tom whether he welcomed questions. Tom thought for a moment and answered, 'Of course I do. If you don't ask questions, you'll never learn.'

The irony of endless questions with no answers was, apparently, completely lost on him.

Advice to Tom

You are a rare species! You appear to be the opposite of the usual gung-ho, shoot-from-the-hip-and-ask-questions-afterwards (if at all!) sort of manager!

Managers who are happy to pose questions and reflect are in a minority.

There is, however, a strange imbalance in your behaviour; your diagnostic skills are clearly not matched by your prescriptive skills. Questions usually pave the way to answers. In your case, we have a surfeit of the former and a shortage of the latter.

Try asking yourself (more questions – you'll be good at this!) why you are asking questions; what objective are you seeking to achieve? Here are a number of possibilities:

1. To gain information/knowledge/insights.

2. To clarify something that isn't clear.

3. To prepare the way to finding answers/solutions to problems.

4. To plant your ideas in a subtle way thus reducing the likelihood of objections.

5. To get people to think things through and discover their own answers.

6. To test out the worthwhileness of an idea by playing devil's advocate.

7. To gently defuse a tricky/volatile situation.

8. To win some thinking time/to conceal the fact that you don't have answers.

9. To impress people with your calm, rational, analytical approach.

As you reflect on these, and other possibilities, you may realise that you have different objectives at different times depending on the circumstances. Sometimes you may be asking questions as a straightforward way of seeking further information/clarification (1 and 2 above). At other times you may be using questions to reduce resistance and plant seeds (3, 4 and 5 above). On other occasions, you might be using questions as a way of testing things (6 above) or as a calming device (7 above). Or, of course, you could be asking questions to win time (8 above) or to demonstrate your prowess at asking insightful questions (9 above).

All of these are perfectly legitimate – so long as they are successful in achieving the desired outcomes. At present, I have the impression that people on the receiving end of your behaviour are somewhat bemused by your persistent questioning – almost, as they would see it, for its own sake.

I recommend that you get into the habit of sending out clearer signals about your intentions. For example, you could easily flag up your objectives by saying things like, 'I just need to clarify this', 'Let's mull this over and see what ideas emerge', 'Here are some questions to take into account as you come up with suggestions', 'Let's play with this for a while and see if it stands up to scrutiny' and 'Hmm ... I don't have an immediate answer but I have some questions to ask.'

Making your objectives more explicit should achieve two useful outcomes. Firstly, people will be less confused and therefore more likely to respond appropriately to your questions. Secondly, you yourself will be clearer as to why you are asking questions and therefore be more purposeful.

Questions are fine so long as they deliver, and it is up to you to get them to work.

7

A manager who liked to keep things simple

Ted was the founder of a firm that made thermostats. He was an engineer by training but his real *forte* was inventing things and patenting the designs. He had personally designed all the thermostats produced by his factory. It was a buoyant business with a full order book and an international reputation.

Ted was the first person in the world to have a thermostat on his car that warned him when the road surface temperature was approaching freezing. He rigged up the prototype himself, positioning the thermostat just behind the front number-plate. His house was full of extraordinary gadgets – all invented by him. He had switches that went on and off at set times long before they became fashionable. Fires sprang into life without human intervention. Curtains would automatically close themselves at dusk and open themselves at dawn. Hot water was supplied by solar panels and the garden gate opened, as if by magic, as you approached it.

Ted had an intense, determined air and a decidedly stubborn streak. One of his mantras was KISS – keep it simple stupid. He had a gift for reducing complicated ideas to the straightforward and understandable. He used to say, 'If it's simple, it'll be practical. If it's practical, it'll be used. If it's used, it'll make a difference.' Time and time again, if someone came to him with a complicated concept, he'd tell them to go away and simplify it.

A long-standing problem in the factory was how to select the people who made the final adjustments to the bi-metal blades (the mechanism inside thermostats that causes them to switch on and off at different temperatures). The final setting of the blades was done by dipping them alternately into twin basins of oil, one at the 'on' temperature and one at the 'off' temperature.

Factory folklore held that it was only women who had the necessary dexterity to do this work. But not *all* women; only some seemed to have the requisite touch. The difficulty was that no one knew how to predict those who possessed the mysterious skill and those who didn't. So over the years a rough and ready protocol had developed whereby anyone (provided they were female!) could have a try. If after two weeks they could set blades fast and accurately enough they were offered the job when next there was a vacancy. If they failed, they simply returned to their normal work with the stigma of rejection. Piece rates for the bi-metal blade setters were the highest in the factory, so competition for the work was fierce.

As you can imagine, this process was divisive and, all too often, caused hopes to be raised then dashed. Ted yearned for some sort of simple test that would identify whether someone had the necessary aptitude and save all the heartache. He contacted the psychology department of the nearest university and set them the challenge.

A graduate researcher from the occupational psychology department started work, confident that the problem could be solved. The researcher, a woman, started by observing the women who could set the blades. They worked fast, moulding the blades between their thumb and first finger while chatting away with their immediate neighbours. Clearly the skill was something to do with eye-hand co-ordination. Next the researcher watched a couple of women who were on trial and she invited back a couple of recent 'failures' and watched them too. Then, with a sample of ten women who could set the blades and ten who couldn't, she set out to find a test that would discriminate between the two groups.

However, all the obvious aptitude tests that should have worked failed. There was no significant difference between the 'coulds' and 'could nots'. Puzzled, the researcher tried an intelligence test, then a personality test. Again, they failed to distinguish between the two groups of women.

Whenever the researcher met Ted he'd ask her cheerfully, 'Got me a simple solution yet?' She didn't dare tell him that the whole thing was proving an elusive puzzle.

Baffled, the researcher talked the problem over with a colleague at the university. They reviewed all the results and wondered what else to try. Over coffee another colleague suggested the dotting test. This involved giving someone a sheet of paper divided into half-inch squares and allowing them 60 seconds to place three dots in as many squares as possible. In comparison with the aptitude tests the researcher had already tried, this seemed absurdly simple and none too promising. Still, since nothing else had produced a result, they decided they might as well try it.

To their amazement, the dotting test proved a triumph. The women who could set the blades succeeded in putting dots in more of the squares than those who couldn't. Incredulous, the researcher tried the test on a bigger population and, sure enough, there was a significant difference between the groups.

The researcher went to Ted with the good news. When Ted heard that the solution to his irksome long-term problem was a 60-second test requiring merely a sheet of paper, a pencil and a stopwatch he became highly agitated.

'What!', he said, 'Are we paying you fees for this? It can't be *that* simple!'

Advice to Ted

Whoops, you forgot your maxim about keeping things simple. It really isn't on to demand simplicity and then, when you are presented with a splendid example, for your first reaction to be dismissive. I can only hope that you made a quick recovery as it dawned on you that the researcher had given you exactly what you wanted; an utterly straightforward solution to a complex problem that had dogged your factory for ages.

Managers are often guilty of espousing principles and values and then failing to walk their own talk. Gaps between rhetoric and behaviour are unfortunately a common occurrence and this causes widespread cynicism about such things as mission statements and other attempts to articulate values, best practice standards and 'the vision thing'. It gives a whole new meaning to the expression 'Mind the gap'.

It might help you to remain consistent with your espoused values if you wrote them down. This might seem like overkill but committing them to paper could be useful in at least two ways. Firstly, it could act as a personal reminder and help to prevent you from blurting out something that you later regret and have to withdraw. Secondly, it would make it easier to share your values with other people so that they are crystal clear where you are coming from. Sharing your values openly has the added advantage of putting yourself under pressure to be consistent. Going public and then being seen to deviate from what you said you were going to do, would make you look foolish or, worse still, hypocritical.

So, if you are serious about your quest to keep things simple, try having a poster on your office wall. It could (simply!) say:

'Simple equals Practical,
Practical equals Useable.'

And, if you haven't already done so, be sure to congratulate the researcher on a job well done. Pay the fees with alacrity and throw in a bonus for coming up with a simple, practical, useable solution.

8

A manager who succumbed to a staff attitude survey

Nigel was a director who managed (he would undoubtedly have said 'led') a factory assembling computers and IT hardware. Most of the staff were women doing fairly intricate work with circuit boards and the like, but, as is so often the way, all the managers and unit heads were men. This suited Nigel very well who, whist he was capable of switching on the charm, was an autocrat through and through. He had little idea of collaboration or even consultation. Decisions, right or wrong, were what he believed he was on this earth to make.

One day Nigel went to a seminar at the Institute of Directors where a speaker waxed lyrical about the benefits of staff attitude surveys and upward feedback. Nigel was attracted by the concept – not for himself, but for his direct reports, many of whom he found wanting. He thought that a dose of upward feedback would help them to see the error of their ways – perhaps even give him an excuse to fire them. So, never having done anything like this before, he hired an outside consultant (from the same firm that the speaker at the Institute had used) to conduct an attitude survey among all the staff.

A detailed questionnaire invited staff, anonymously, to say what they thought about everything from the food in the canteen to the quality of their managers. The staff, not used to being consulted or listened to, relished the opportunity to have their say. Accordingly, the response rate was over 90 per cent – the highest ever in the consultant's experience of conducting surveys of this kind.

The questionnaires were analysed and the consultant went to see Nigel to give him a preliminary overview of the data prior to its being fed back to the whole management group. The consultant said, 'There is a great deal of detail to go through, but I can summarise the findings by telling you that the majority of your staff are very critical of management in general and you in particular. In fact, not to put too fine a point on it, they think you are an out and out bastard.'

Nigel was shocked to hear this. He was sufficiently self-aware to appreciate that he was dictatorial, but he had always seen himself as a benevolent autocrat, making decisions in the interests of his workforce. How could he be so seriously misunderstood?

The consultant, used to dealing with senior managers in a state of denial when confronted with their feedback, reassured Nigel that this was not at all unusual. He said he would be delighted to help Nigel put together a plan that would change the staff's perceptions for the better. The plan was simple. For one year, Nigel would spend one hour each working day talking with staff, asking for their ideas and being seen to listen. After the year, the staff attitude survey would be repeated so that the improvement could be measured.

The consultant coached Nigel in the skills of active listening, with all the verbal and non-verbal behaviours necessary to convince people he really was listening.

So for a year Nigel applied his charm and, supported by the consultant, diligently implemented the plan. He was genuinely surprised by the quality of the ideas that were forthcoming from his staff. Some of them resulted directly in cost-saving efficiencies. During the year he was also able to prevent a strike that would almost certainly have happened but for the plan to consult widely. All in all, Nigel felt pleased with himself.

The time came to repeat the attitude survey and analyse the results. Again, the response rate was high and, again, the consultant met with Nigel to review the trends.

The consultant said, 'As you know, there is a great deal of detail to go through, but I am pleased to tell you there has been some improvement. The majority of your staff now think you are a *cunning* bastard!'

Advice to Nigel

People aren't stupid. Switching on the charm for an hour a day isn't going to convince your staff that you are no longer an autocratic bastard. In fact, the contrast between actively listening for an hour a day and the way you undoubtedly behave during the other seven hours at work, must seem very comical. Surely you didn't seriously imagine that your staff would fall for such a transparent ploy?

The sudden switch from being consultative to being autocratic and back again, must mean that people are suspicious of your motives. They'll be in no doubt that you are fundamentally an autocrat and that the short spells of consultation are forced and artificial. Quite understandably, your staff will doubt that you are being genuine.

Despite these problems, I'm pleased to hear that you have discovered that, when you listen to your staff, some worthwhile ideas are forthcoming. You have proved, in your clumsy way, that consultation actually works!

I strongly recommend that you give some thought to deciding which management style best fits the circumstances you are facing. *Always* being autocratic or *always* being consultative cannot possibly *always* be appropriate. You need to be clear when to be autocratic and when to be democratic. Here is a simple guide.

An autocratic 'telling' approach tends to be appropriate when:

- You are better informed and more experienced than the others who are involved (i.e. you literally know best).

- The task is close-ended (i.e. there is a right answer or a precedent that needs to be upheld).

- A decision needs to be taken quickly/urgently.

- You need to exert tight control and minimise the likelihood of mistakes.

- Large numbers of people are involved (i.e. seeking a consensus would be unwieldy).

- Genuine buy-in would be nice but it is not absolutely essential (you have to accept that some people will only comply grudgingly).

A democratic 'asking' approach tends to work best when:

- Other people know at least as much, if not more, than you do.

- The task is open-ended (i.e. there are options to choose between).

- There is time to explore the options and reach a consensus.

- The risks of getting it wrong first time round are not unacceptably high (i.e. there will be subsequent opportunities to review and refine).

- The number of people involved is manageable.

- Buy-in and genuine commitment is essential to the success of the chosen course of action.

So, you are right to vary your style, but not by the clock; more by weighing up the ingredients of the situation you are facing. A useful technique to allay people's suspicions that you are playing games, is to be transparent about why you have decided to adopt a particular style. This is easy if you have used the above checklists to reach a decision. Simply flag up your decision by saying something like, 'We need to move fast, so I'll do the talking', 'I have faced this situation many times before, so I'll tell you what we need to do', 'I'm interested in your views, so I'll keep quiet and do the listening', 'There are many possibilities here, let's explore the options.'

Straightforward announcements like these send a clear signal to people and help them to understand where you are coming from. I'll guarantee that if you follow this advice consistently over a period of time, your staff will no longer perceive you as a cunning bastard – perhaps not even as a bastard at all!

9

A manager with a reputation for being calm and unruffled

Gordon was a senior partner in a law firm. He was a qualified solicitor and headed a small team of lawyers specialising in employment law. Employers anxious to avoid tribunal hearings, or to win them, drew heavily on Gordon's considerable expertise. He kept abreast of every nuance of employment law – national, European and international – and was totally at home reading pages of small print and making copious notes in the margins. Such was Gordon's reputation that his views were often sought by civil servants when writing briefs for ministers or drafting new legislation.

Gordon was a quietly spoken, mild mannered man who had never been known to become ruffled or lose his temper. Indeed, he was famous for exuding a calm air of rationality no matter what. Sometimes Gordon's colleagues would mischievously test his patience to see if they could provoke him. But Gordon always remained calm, displaying no hint of irritation – or even any sign that he realised he was being teased! He would gaze at them through his thick lenses, nod his head sagely, and give a measured opinion. If asked to repeat it, he would do so patiently as if reassuring someone threatening to jump off a high ledge.

One day Gordon had a client who was particularly trying. He was an HR director from an organisation that was downsizing and coming under fire from the unions who represented their staff. The situation was very fraught. A programme of compulsory redundancies had been announced and there were many tricky disputes to resolve. Quite understandably, the HR director, who had never experienced such a crisis before, and was under pressure from his bosses to find ways to limit the damage, was feeling nervous. It was as though he was paralysed by fear. He'd ask the same question over and over again – invariably starting with the words, 'With all due respect …'. And Gordon would keep cool and calmly reiterate the answers as if he were saying them for the first time.

Gordon followed up each meeting with a detailed written summary of the points covered sent as an email attachment. But that only unleashed a spate of emails listing detailed queries and questions of clarification. Characteristically, Gordon would deal with them all with the utmost care.

At the fourth meeting with this particular client, Gordon, together with three members of his team, once again faced the twitchy HR director. Hearts sank as they realised he needed to go over everything again for the umpteenth time.

After the sixth 'With all due respect', Gordon leant forward and said quietly, 'May I offer you some feedback?'. The client looked surprised but gave a slight, almost imperceptible, nod of the head. Gordon leaned even further forward until the tips of their noses nearly touched. Suddenly he yelled, 'You piss me off!'

After years of rigorous self-control, poor Gordon had finally exploded.

Advice to Gordon

I'm tempted to say good for you! It sounds as if you have been remarkably patient under trying circumstances. I hope you now feel better having unloaded some of those bottled up frustrations. The straw has finally broken the camel's back!

However, I'd question the wisdom of suppressing your feelings and letting your frustration build up to such a pitch. Think of a wedge. At the thin end, when your client first started to behave in ways that you found trying, you only felt mildly irritated. At this stage it is easy to grin and bear it and say nothing. In the absence of any feedback, the client continues to irritate you, and your mild frustration now becomes intense. But you remind yourself that this is an important client, and soldier on as if everything is fine. The behaviour continues and things progress to the thick end of the wedge. Now you are feeling incensed and it takes a super human effort not to let this show.

There is a simple tactic that can come to your rescue in future. It works best when you are still at the thin end of the wedge.

As soon as you feel irritated with someone's behaviour, say so. Don't delay and let things fester. To do so will only allow things to escalate as they climb up the wedge. Say something assertive such as, 'When you say 'with respect' it really irritates me. I'd prefer it if you just said what you want to say in a straightforward manner.'

This example provides a useful 'formula' that you can adapt to suit different circumstances. The first part of the statement identifies the behaviour you want the other person to discontinue. This must be confined to their behaviour, i.e. something they either say or do. It is not a criticism of them as a person. The second part is an open and honest declaration about how you feel on the receiving end of the behaviour. The final part makes it clear what you want.

I'm sure you will find it helpful to assert your grievance and, even more importantly, what you want them to change early on before things escalate and your resentment grows. I'm therefore recommending a pre-emptive strike. Not only does this stand a good chance of nipping the irritating behaviour in the bud, it will also help you to feel better about yourself for getting on top of the situation and handling it well.

10

A manager who showed his frustration in an unusual way

Dave was a director of a division in a large IT company. Young and ambitious, he had a reputation for being brilliant but impetuous and unpredictable. He certainly didn't suffer fools gladly and quickly became exasperated if anyone was slow to grasp the point – a frequent occurrence since he threw out his points with inadequate explanation or context.

The CEO of the company, Dave's boss, decided that his directors should be better at chairing meetings and he arranged for an external consultant to observe some meetings run by directors and give instant feedback. The unfortunate Dave was chosen as one of the guinea pigs and it was agreed that the consultant would attend one of his regular team meetings.

When the day came to visit Dave, the consultant arrived early to say hello, explain his mission and receive a briefing on the meeting he was about to watch. The consultant was delighted to learn that they were facing a tricky situation with a trade union and had decided to abandon their customary team meeting and instead use the occasion to examine their options and agree their negotiating strategy. This sounded far more interesting than observing Dave's team going through their routine agenda.

The consultant took up position in a corner of the room, behind a handy rubber plant. The meeting began, with Dave doing most of the talking. After a while, he grabbed a pencil and thrust it into the jaws of a battery-driven pencil sharpener and held it there until it had all but disappeared. The consultant thought this an odd behaviour, noted the time, and entered it in his log. Three minutes later Dave threw a tantrum. As he ranted and raved (about lack of progress, that no one was helping him, that he was having to think up all the ideas himself, that everyone was spineless, etc.) his colleagues kept quiet and waited for him to calm down. After a short while, the storm blew over and the meeting went on as if nothing had happened.

This pattern – grind a pencil to destruction, wait three minutes, go berserk – repeated itself three times before it was time to adjourn for lunch.

A couple of the participants took the consultant to lunch in the staff canteen where they regaled him with stories about Dave's unpredictable outbursts. The consultant was suitably circumspect and confined himself to occasional noncommittal 'hms'. At last, however, he ventured an observation. He said he thought there was a link between a pencil being sharpened and, three minutes later, a ranting and raving episode. The theory was that the pencil sharpening was a signal that Dave's frustration was building up – in effect, a three-minute warning. The consultant was pleased when his two lunchtime colleagues marvelled at this striking insight!

The meeting reconvened after the lunch break and after a while (you've guessed, haven't you?) Dave seized a pencil and ground it down into a pile of shavings. Unfortunately the two managers who had lunched with the consultant turned towards his rubber plant and one winked knowingly and the other gave the consultant a quick grin. Dave saw this and didn't wait the customary three minutes before exploding. He demanded an instant explanation. Heads went down and no explanation was forthcoming. So the consultant gallantly admitted that it was his fault and explained that over lunch he had advanced the theory that pencil sharpening was an early indication of frustration with the lack of progress.

Everyone went pale at the consultant's audacity (no one had ever dared to broach so sensitive a subject with Dave). Dave looked livid and asked the consultant to wait behind afterwards. Naturally, the consultant feared that his career was at an end.

When the meeting finished and the last person had left, Dave closed the door and said, 'That was a very interesting observation. Having watched me in action, what other feedback can you offer me?' For the next hour he lapped up all the feedback the consultant could offer and thanked him profusely for his candour and help.

Many weeks later the consultant saw Dave in passing and asked him if he was still sharpening pencils. 'Yes', he said cheerfully, 'but now I know why I'm doing it.'

Advice to Dave

Just think what you could learn if you were open to some honest feedback! You'd discover, for example, that your staff regard your habit of sharpening pencils and throwing wobblies as a joke. More importantly, feedback would help you see that your frequent tantrums do nothing to improve the effectiveness of your staff. Very sensibly, they just put their heads down and wait for you to recover your decorum!

Under the circumstances, it is entirely understandable why you are starved of feedback. Your subordinates hold back for fear of incurring your wrath, and, since you are a senior director, the chances are that your boss and colleagues fail to offer you any helpful feedback either. A lack of feedback about your management style, makes it well nigh impossible for you decide what, if anything, to modify. No feedback, no learning.

The interest you showed in the feedback extracted from the consultant offers a ray of hope. However, if the feedback you receive only serves to increase your self-awareness (and/or to stroke your ego!) without any commensurate adjustments to your behaviour, then there is no point in proceeding. You must be prepared to act on the feedback.

There are a number of initiatives you could take to solicit useful feedback from your colleagues.

First, try asking for it! This may seem obvious – but it is surprising how rarely feedback is explicitly invited. Always ask for specific feedback on something you have done recently. So, for example, ask for ideas on how you could chair meetings so that they accomplished their purpose more quickly and/or with less hassle. Initially you should expect people to be guarded. However, if you persevere, you'll gradually find the feedback becomes more candid and illuminating.

Second, you could indulge in a more formal upward feedback exercise. This could be anonymous (to encourage the faint hearted and to prevent you 'shooting the messenger'!). Keep it simple by asking your staff what they would like you to a) do more of and b) do less of. Feedback from different people, with their different points of view, will inevitably be contradictory. You can survive this by looking for the common denominators, or trends, running through the feedback.

Whether you gather feedback informally or formally, remember that you are the final arbiter. You, as the person who 'owns' the feedback, need to decide what to accept and act upon, and what to discard or ignore.

If you don't like the feedback, resist the temptation to spring to your own defence or to become argumentative. Stick to asking for clarification so that you can understand the other person's point of view. It is always worth collecting specific examples of things you have done or not done.

Finally, thank the person giving you feedback and say you'll give serious consideration to what they've said.

11

A manager who was democratic to a fault

Walter was a professor of psychology at a red-brick university. In many ways he fitted the stereotype of a psychology professor; he was a short, cuddly man, with thick spectacles and two front teeth that protruded over his bottom lip, making him look remarkably like a rabbit. He always wore a cardigan, complete with leather elbow patches, which he frequently buttoned up so that the two sides were out of alignment. He kept a pair of carpet slippers in his office and, when the weather was cold and wet, he would put them on and shuffle around the department looking as if he should be wearing pyjamas to match. Even when he put his slippers aside and dressed up for a special occasion, he managed to look scruffy. His tie would sag, his Hush Puppies would be scuffed, his braces would show and, invariably, a label would be sticking out at the back of his neck.

Walter's office was similarly untidy. On his desk sat a phrenological china bust overseeing a mass of dishevelled papers (incongruously there was a little segment marked 'order' over the left eye!). The drawers of his filing cabinet were overflowing. The floor beside the bookcase was littered with stacks of books. There were strange bits of apparatus left over from various laboratory experiments – cardboard shapes painted in different colours, bells rigged up with wires attached to batteries, headphones and loudspeakers. Walter was a wood carver in his spare time, so various wooden bowls and animals also graced the scene.

51

As you might have gathered, Walter was a disorganised man. He was, however, very kindly. He always had time for his staff and the students in the department. If someone came to him with a query or a problem, he would sit them down (after moving whatever was on the chair!) and, unhurriedly, talk through all the issues. He was extraordinarily circumlocutory because he subscribed to the non-directive school of thought. He rarely gave a direct answer, preferring to skirt round the edges of a topic, asking many questions – often rhetorical – and repeating himself needlessly. He firmly believed that his role was to act as a sounding board and allow his colleagues to reach their own decisions in their own time. This meant that the faculty meetings he chaired were rambling, inconclusive affairs, taking far more time than was necessary.

One day Walter told the meeting that the university was to enter into an arrangement with the city's art gallery whereby paintings would be loaned to the university for a period of time. Each department could join the scheme and have up to three paintings on loan for a six-month period. They would then be rotated and replaced with another three paintings, and so on for as long as the arrangement stood.

Walter liked the idea but, of course, refrained from saying so openly and waited for a consensus to emerge. Members of the faculty fell into two camps; those with an interest in art who were keen and those with no interest in art who couldn't care less. Eventually, it was decided there was no harm in going ahead and Walter conveyed the decision to the University's Vice Chancellor.

At the next meeting, Walter produced a catalogue showing twelve paintings. Walter suggested that they should use a democratic process to choose their first three paintings. A long discussion ensued about how this could best be done. The group that were not interested saw this as an opportunity to have fun and use spoiling tactics to make things difficult. In the end, it was decided to circulate the catalogue so that everyone could make their individual choices, returning it to Walter in time for him to announce the result at the next faculty meeting.

When the catalogue came back, marked with everyone's choices, Walter was dismayed to see that the votes were spread more or less evenly among all twelve paintings and that no clear consensus had emerged. He wondered what to do for the best. Perhaps he should just go ahead and choose the three paintings himself? But it was against his principles to ignore the vote and ride roughshod over the opinions of his colleagues. Perhaps he should quietly take some individuals aside and persuade them to change their votes? But that amounted to rigging the vote and leaving him open to accusations of unfairness. Perhaps he should drop the whole idea? But how would he explain the change of heart to the Vice Chancellor? There was nothing for it but to feed back the inconclusive data at the next meeting and explore views on the best way ahead.

Before the meeting, Walter felt strangely apprehensive. He normally took such problems in his stride, happy to let them resolve themselves, trusting that democracy would find a way, but this time he was in the grip of cognitive dissonance. On the eve of the meeting, Walter had a particularly restless night with a vivid dream about *The Scream* being stolen whilst on loan to his department!

The next day, poor Walter arrived looking even more dishevelled than usual. Nervously, he broke the news about the impasse and asked for ideas on how best to proceed. After some discussion about whether to have a second round of voting with some form of proportional representation, one of the lecturers put forward a novel idea. She suggested that the task of deciding on the three paintings should be delegated to a sub-committee. This led to a discussion about the ideal number for a sub-committee. Eventually, it was decided that three would suffice – one for each painting. However, when Walter asked for volunteers, everyone clamoured to join. The people who didn't care were playing games again.

After a while, the lecturer who had suggested the sub-committee (she was in favour of having paintings) said, 'Professor, in the circumstances, I think that you should make the decision and we should all agree to abide by it.' By now everyone, even the mischief-makers, was growing tired of the discussion and the prevaricating, so the idea went through on the nod.

Walter chose the paintings happy in the knowledge that the decision to let him do so had been reached democratically. He reflected that, although it had all been rather tortuous, democracy had triumphed yet again. Consonance was restored.

Advice to Walter

I don't like the sound of those rambling, inconclusive faculty meetings you chair. Generally speaking meetings enjoy a bad press and it seems that yours are no exception. Common complaints are that meetings:

- gobble up too much time;

- are boring;

- go round in circles;

- lack a clear purpose or objective;

- suffer from inadequate preparation;

- have an over ambitious agenda (or, by contrast, have no agenda at all!).

However, the biggest single complaint is that meetings are poorly chaired. This is partly because the chair is a natural scapegoat – it is easy for people who have behaved badly in a meeting to blame the chair for not having kept a grip on discipline. But, it is also because most meetings are in fact chaired badly.

The challenge of chairing a meeting effectively is invariably underestimated. It is a tough assignment with many different aspects competing for simultaneous attention. The structure of the meeting, time management, clear communications, sound decision-making processes, orderly behaviour, as well as the quality of the content of the meeting, are all aspects of the meeting over which the chairperson has considerable influence. Undoubtedly the biggest mistake is to assume that it is possible to manage all these processes whilst becoming heavily involved in the subject matter of the meeting. It simply isn't possible simultaneously to wear two hats – a 'task' hat and a 'process' hat. The temptation is for the chair to become engrossed in the subject matter and give the processes of the meeting insufficient attention. Unless the participants are unusually good at self-regulation, this is when things start to slip.

So, I think you should focus on your chairing skills and tighten your grip on your faculty meetings. I'm sure you will have reservations about this because of your insistence on using a non-directive approach. This may be appropriate when counselling someone on a one-to-one basis, but it is likely to be disastrous when chairing meetings – especially if you have some participants who are hell bent on being mischievous!

Here are ten suggestions for you – but please tackle only one at a time. When you have successfully implemented one, you can progress to the next and so on until you have mastered them all.

- Have an agenda for each meeting with an objective and time slot for each item.

- Start the meeting punctually at the advertised time (even if some participants are absent)

- Introduce each agenda item by clarifying whether it is 'for information', 'for consultation', or 'for decision'.

- Keep the meeting on track and ensure that each agenda item keeps within its allotted time.

- Focus on the 'hows' of the meeting rather than getting directly involved in the subject matter. If you 'own' the subject matter, get someone else to chair that agenda item.

- Conclude each topic by summarising what has been

agreed/decided.

- Actively invite contributions from the quieter participants and restrain the noisier ones.

- Check that, as a consequence of the meeting, everyone knows exactly who is supposed to do what, and by when.

- Ask participants for their ideas on how the next meeting could be improved.

- Immediately after the meeting, circulate a list of actions with the names of those responsible beside each.

If you implement even half of these, your faculty meetings will be transformed.

12

A manager who was wedded to short-termism

Jim was the CEO of a company that designed and manufactured packaging of all shapes and sizes. Their products embraced all the latest technology and included advanced plastics, bubble wrap, polystyrene and different sorts of pliable cardboard (they called it 'intelligent' cardboard, almost certainly a contradiction in terms).

Jim was one of those who, every waking moment, exhibit such boundless energy and enthusiasm that it is impossible to believe they are genuine. A large man, slightly overweight, with a florid complexion, one couldn't help but think that he was a prime candidate for an early heart attack. When you met him he would bound forward with a huge smile on his face and a big hand outstretched. His handshake was vigorous and his eye contact unflinching. He talked loud and fast. You were left in no doubt that this man was in command. He exuded charisma.

Jim's philosophy can be summed up with just one three-letter word: now. He never tired of telling people that life was just one now after another. Past 'nows' had gone and there was nothing you could do about them. Future 'nows' lay ahead, were not even guaranteed, and were full of unknowns. The only certainty was your current reality – now.

Jim even knew how many seconds there were in a day and on his office wall he had a framed poster which read:

Imagine a bank that credits your current account each morning with £86,400. At the end of each 24-hour period it deletes the balance you haven't used and credits you with the next instalment of £86,400.

You have such a bank. Its name is time. Every morning it credits you with 86,400 seconds. It carries over no balance. It allows no overdraft. It is up to you to use the daily balance.

Yesterday is history. Tomorrow is mystery. Today is a gift – that's why it's called the present.

This approach to life meant that Jim refused to dwell on the past, not even on the recent past such as what happened yesterday. He just pressed on, refusing to entertain any regrets or guilt (he claimed that guilt was pointless – the equivalent of worrying backwards).

The 'now' philosophy had, however, an unexpected effect on Jim's approach to the future. You might have expected that he would condemn planning for the future, with all its uncertainties, as a waste of precious 'now' time. On the contrary, Jim saw planning as a legitimate 'now' activity – a sensible investment in shaping the pattern of future 'nows'. Admittedly, he was only prepared to contemplate the near future. He had a three-month time horizon; anything beyond that was a stretch too far. 'In the long run,' he'd say cheerfully, 'we're all dead.' So he refused to waste precious 'now' time on things like a long-term strategy or a five-year business plan. A three-month rolling plan was fine; anything longer-term was futile.

Jim treated everything as a campaign, with a clear beginning and end. The idea of continuity bored him. In fact, Jim's determination to treasure every second meant that he had an abnormally low boredom threshold. If nothing exciting was happening, then he'd find a way to stir things up.

59

If, for example, he was talking to a person he found boring, he'd suddenly ask them a disconcerting question such as, 'What's the worst thing that has ever happened to you?' Or, 'How do you feel about squirrels?' Or, 'How's your sex life?' Jim found that people's reactions to unexpected questions like these made conversations much more interesting. Some people would take offence and refuse to answer (*always* interesting!), some would look surprised but manage an answer, others would happily lurch into an amusing anecdote.

Campaigns, Jim maintained, kept staff focused and gave them a sense of urgency. It wasn't that he'd reject continuous improvement, say, or quality circles, just that he'd prefer to break the activities involved into chunks and make each chunk a campaign. Jim usually thought of ideas for campaigns while shaving, and by the time he reached his office the idea would have crystallised and Jim would be eager to start. A campaign with a small 'c' could last for as short a time as a week. Examples were to ask everyone to smile, to clear the site of litter, to greet customers in person or on the phone with the words 'How may I help?', to limit the length of documents to one side of A4, to limit the number of emails sent to colleagues to a maximum of five per day ... and so on. Campaigns with a big 'C', lasting for up to twelve weeks (Jim's horizon!), tackled more substantial issues such as how to make meetings more productive (halve the length, double the actions), how to reduce waste, how to speed up decision making, how to introduce flexitime, how to increase the autonomy of teams.

Jim was blissfully happy, improvising as he went along. Until, that is, the chairman of the company retired and a new one took over. The old chairman had been happy to abdicate responsibility to Jim – anything for an easy life. But the new man, unfortunately for Jim, was keen on strategy (he even talked of strategic leadership!) and one of the first things he wanted to review was the five-year business plan. This, of course, did not exist.

Jim did his best to explain the 'now' philosophy with all its advantages – innovation, flexibility, being nimble in the face of change, keeping people fresh and on their toes. But the new chairman frowned and shook his head. 'Jim,' he said, 'you're making an erroneous assumption.'

He tended to use words like erroneous. At first Jim thought he was saying erogenous – a far more interesting notion – but, sadly, he soon realised the chairman meant what he said.

'You see,' he continued, 'the point of strategic planning is to have something to change, not to have something to implement. The key to being nimble is to have a plan that you can quickly adapt in the light of changed circumstances that you couldn't predict. It takes much longer if you have to start from scratch each time.'

Jim looked puzzled. 'If the proof of a pudding is in the eating, I thought the proof of a plan was in its implementation.'

'Absolutely not,' said the chairman, refusing to budge. 'I'm afraid you've missed the point. Plans are nothing, planning is everything.'

Jim moved from looking puzzled to looking doubtful. The chairman then made a tactical error (he might have thought it was strategic!). He said, 'Planning is *always* work in progress. It is everlasting. It never ends.'

When Jim heard that the chairman expected him to indulge in an endless activity, he decided there and then to embark on a new campaign; to find himself another job – preferably one where a talent for short-termism would be appropriate and appreciated.

61

Advice to Jim

You and your chairman are both half right (or both half wrong depending on your point of view!). Both short-term tactics and long-term strategy matter. But what matters even more is the connection between the two.

Current actions (you'd call them 'nows') are best shaped with an eye on longer term considerations – otherwise you risk finishing up with a mishmash of tactics that lack any coherence. I suspect that your numerous campaigns may well be an example of this.

Possibly the only real difference of opinion between you and your chairman is over the time frame; how long *is* long-term? Your horizon is set at three months and your chairman's at five years. Clearly the longer the time frame the greater the uncertainties and the more hazardous the forecasts about what might happen. Your chairman's way of coping with this uncertainty is to treat plans as malleable things that require constant adjustment in the face of unexpected events. You, with your shorter time span, and therefore fewer uncertainties, tend to regard plans as 'fixtures'. This means you are likely to consider it some sort of indictment if a plan has to be adapted during its lifetime.

I think you'd feel happier about extending your time horizon if you remembered that the best way to predict the future is to invent it. You need to distinguish between a *predicted* future and a *preferred* future. A predicted future is where you extrapolate from what has happened in the past and predict a likely continuing trend. This is relatively unadventurous and assumes that what has happened in the past will, more or less, continue to happen in the future. It reinforces the maxim 'If you always do what you've always done, you'll always get what you've always got.'

A *preferred* future is quite different. This is where you forget about trends and extrapolations. You even put aside today's obstacles and constraints and, in a liberated, 'blue-sky' state, you ask yourself, 'What do I *want* to exist in (five years) time?'. This gives you an exciting vision of a preferred future which is far removed from where you are now. Then, with this goal firmly in mind, you plan some first steps to get you started on the long journey from your current reality to your preferred reality. After the first steps have been taken, you review progress towards the goal and plan the next few steps. And so on. This ensures that the short-term plans are coherent, or 'joined up', and designed to make steady progress towards your preferred state.

Why not try it by casting yourself forward just one year? I appreciate that this still won't satisfy your chairman, but at least it is a move in the right direction. You can gradually extend the time scale as you become more comfortable with envisaging future 'nows'.

By the way, it is infinitely preferable to involve your colleagues in the visioning activity. An *agreed* preferred future gets buy-in and helps to ensure that all the steps are moving in the right direction. Invite your chairman to join in and watch your differences evaporate.

13
A manager who lapsed into long silences

Bill was a senior manager in a large telecommunications company. There was a studious air about him. He wore spectacles with thick lenses that magnified his eyes. Bald and portly, he was always well turned out – never succumbing to the invitation to dress down on Fridays – and his shoes were exceptionally highly polished. In a previous existence he had been an army officer and retained the practice of polishing his shoes with a soft cloth (never anything so rough as a brush!) and much spit and polish.

Bill had one truly alarming habit; without warning, in the middle of a conversation, he would fall silent. There were many occasions when he was talking over a project with a colleague when, suddenly, Bill would lapse into silence. This could happen at any time – in mid-sentence, when you had finished answering a question he had put to you, even when you asked him a question.

Once Bill had stopped, it was as though he had gone into suspended animation. He'd gaze at you through those big lenses with a blank expression. If he had been a character in a comic, he'd have been drawn with a stream of 'thinks' bubbles emanating from the top of his head. In the absence of any bubbles, it was hard for anyone to know how to interpret the sudden silence. Had something offended him? Had he lost his train of thought? Had he been asked a question that was so profound that it required deep thought? Had he been struck dumb by a stroke?

One of Bill's colleagues became very irritated with his own inability to tolerate the silences. The first few times Bill inflicted a sudden silence on him, in common with most people, he would obligingly fill the gap by making some comment. In hindsight, he always regretted this because it meant he had blurted out inconsequential, ill-advised statements just to fill the silence.

So the colleague devised a plan to survive the silences. He set himself the objective of not, under any circumstances, being the next to speak. No matter how long it took, Bill would have to break the silence, not him. The plan to survive the silence was simple (as the best plans always are); he would concentrate on counting (not sheep, but numbers!) and this, he reckoned, would give him something to do to fill the void.

He only had to implement his plan once. Bill fell silent, the colleague started counting (in his head, not out loud). He kept counting, and counting, and counting. Eventually, somewhere in the three-hundreds, Bill broke the silence by saying, 'You've changed.'

The colleague told him about his plan and Bill never inflicted a silence on him again.

Advice to Bill

Let's face it, you've been rumbled! Your ploy of lapsing into sudden silences will no longer work. The colleague who broke the pattern by counting his way through the silence, will surely pass this on to your other victims. If they have any sense, they'll all start doing it and any advantage you thought you had gained will vanish.

I take it that you adopted the silence routine because you discovered that it was a good way to get people to reveal things that would otherwise be left unsaid? Or perhaps it just amused you to see how different people would cope under pressure? The way you are using silences at present is a form of harassment and bullying.

You needn't totally abandon silences; you just need to throw in an open-ended question *before* becoming silent in anticipation of an expansive answer. Questions are a far better way to get people to open up than silences alone, and they have the added advantage of providing some focus to the discussion. You can control the whole conversation through a few well-placed questions.

In an odd sort of way, your ability to stay silent should stand you in good stead when it comes to listening to the answers to your questions without interrupting. Too many managers make the mistake of jumping in and answering their own questions or cutting people off before they have finished. You are well equipped to avoid these perils.

14

A manager who was desperate to keep in touch

Alex was the managing director of a large bank. He had been wedded to a hierarchical organisation structure and a command-and-control management style all his working life. He had read about matrix management and project management and the like, but found it difficult to see how they would work in the bank, where tight controls were necessary. He had also heard about empowering employees and had read the book *Maverick* with increasing disbelief. The idea of giving employees flexibility and room for manoeuvre and trusting them not to abuse it was beyond his comprehension.

In common with many senior managers of his age and background, he harboured a deep-seated dread of anything that smacked of anarchy. People had to do what they were told and follow laid-down procedures and that was that. The same philosophy extended to his home life, where all was tidy and regulated. One glance at his lawn told the entire story – weed-free, smooth as a bowling green, with straight stripes and clipped edges. His wife, luckily, shared his values. She was house-proud to a fault (teddy bears arranged just so on the ottoman, fresh *potpourri* in a bowl in the hall, orchids on the piano) and insisted on everything being kept in its proper place.

Alex appreciated that if he was to retain control he needed to know what was going on in the bank. In the rarefied atmosphere of his office on the top floor of the headquarters building, he recognised the danger of losing touch. Of course, his colleagues fed him with information and kept him updated, but he suspected that by the time the information reached him it had been heavily censored and filtered as it passed up through the various hierarchical levels.

This worried him. He feared a Nick Leeson-style catastrophe. Yet the bank was too big for Alex to be everywhere, keeping an eye on everything personally – a most unnerving realisation for a control-freak. So he invented 'Skip Level Meetings' (SLMs). The idea was as follows: Each week, Alex would visit a different part of the bank and hold an informal hour-long session with a group of staff at least two levels below him in the hierarchy. The immediate manager of the selected group (the 'father') and his manager (the 'grandfather') were not allowed to be present. There would be no agenda – just an 'anything goes/off-the-record' question-and-answer session. Alex was convinced that these gatherings would, at least partially, solve the problem of how to keep in touch.

From Alex's point of view, the first few SLMs were a great success. Once the staff had recovered from the initial shock of finding themselves face to face with the MD, they quickly appreciated that this was a heaven-sent opportunity to make a favourable impression. They soon appreciated the sort of things he wanted to hear – some relatively harmless examples of inadequate attention to detail, some vague complaints about inadequate communications, some grumbling about poor response times from the IT department and some mild criticisms of pay and conditions.

Alex, however, was *very* pleased with the process. As far as he was concerned, Skip Level Meetings were keeping him in touch and successfully circumventing the filters put in place by two or more levels of management. After each meeting, Alex summoned the relevant management team to feedback his findings and leave them in no doubt that things had to improve.

Predictably, managers in the bank below Alex (in other words, *all* the managers!) became very nervous about SLMs. They resented (a) their exclusion from the meetings with their staff and (b) the reprimands that inevitably followed in the wake of each meeting. A few of the wilier managers began to hold rehearsals, where questions and answers (particularly answers) were practised over and over until the manager was satisfied that the right 'everything-is-under-control' image was being conveyed.

It quickly became clear that rehearsed SLMs led to less subsequent anguish than unrehearsed SLMs. Soon, all the managers were taking precautionary steps. Unbeknown to Alex, hours were spent in rehearsals – hours that could otherwise have been productive.

And all to sustain the illusion that Alex was in touch and in control.

Advice to Alex

You certainly have some deep-seated beliefs about the importance of keeping in touch and maintaining order and control. In common with many managers, you hold an essentially pessimistic view of human nature. Basically, you are assuming that people are neither willing nor able to exercise self-control and that, without your interventions, anarchy would prevail.

I can quite understand why you think Skip Level Meetings are a triumph. Each revelation offered by the staff you meet reinforces your conviction that your managers are withholding the truth and engaged in cover-ups. But has it occurred to you that the staff too, not just the managers, have a vested interest in being economical with the truth? It is in their interests to feed you just enough information to keep you happy – preferably without undermining the working relationship they have with their immediate managers.

I'm sure it will strike you as an unpalatable thought, but the plain truth is that, in a large organisation such as yours, it is impossible for you to know what is *really* going on. All you can hope to do is just stay a little bit in touch. Anything else is illusory. People below you in the hierarchy decide every day what work gets done and how it is done. This is why it is better to create an environment where people are encouraged to take responsibility for their actions, rather than one where people aren't trusted and continually subjected to checks. Command and control approaches tend to stifle initiative and produce defensive people anxious to protect their backs.

In the circumstances, bearing in mind that you are chaos-averse, I recommend that you make only incremental changes to your existing practices. I suspect anything more would be vetoed by you as too risky.

So, how about making the following adjustments to your Skip Level Meetings?

Firstly, make them less 'special' by increasing their frequency and giving less notice. Lowering the profile will help people get used to talking candidly with you. With increasing familiarity, they will become more forthcoming and less guarded.

Secondly, invite the relevant managers to participate in the process. This is vital because leaving them out of the loop makes them resentful and resistant. Their buy-in is vital when implementing improvements as a result of the feedback generated by the meetings. Excluding the managers is a snub – it sends out a message that they are superfluous to requirements.

Thirdly, make it a rule that you will never involve yourself directly in implementing actions after the meetings. Give the responsibility to an appropriate manager. Simply ask to be informed when the action has been taken.

Finally, draw up some ground rules to encourage candour in your Skip Level Meetings. For example, make it clear they are a blame-free zone – people can be open and honest without fear of recrimination. When criticisms are voiced, ban defensive behaviour by insisting that any aggrieved parties confine themselves to asking questions of clarification. Stick to the ground rules come what may.

Hopefully, introducing these modifications will enhance the meetings and make it more likely that people will grow in confidence and take more responsibility. It's up to you to create the climate that will allow these things to happen. Who knows, you might even discover that people are more trustworthy than you had previously believed!

15

A manager who couldn't admit he was still learning

Sir Philip was the chairman of a large financial institution. He led a comfortable, orderly existence. A dapper man with a fine head of white hair parted on the left, he had never been known to raise his voice and was always charming and attentive. Sir Philip exuded an air of calm confidence.

He looked every inch a company chairman. He always wore immaculate pin-striped suits, tasteful ties, gold cuff links, and highly polished shoes. He had an endearing way of gazing at you over the top of his half-moon spectacles. He rose early each morning, let the dogs out, showered, shaved and dressed before being collected from his home in Berkshire at precisely 07:15 by a chauffeur in a company limousine. Before leaving he would take his wife of 40 years a cup of lemon tea and kiss her fondly on the forehead. He always sat in the back of the car as it cruised effortlessly along the M4, with the reading light on so that he could peruse *The Financial Times* (ready for him on the back seat) and look at other documents in preparation for the day ahead.

Once at work, Sir Philip would wish the receptionist a cheery good morning, comment favourably on the display of fresh flowers on the counter, and take the lift to the top floor. His office was spacious with fine views across the City. His breakfast would always be ready on the sideboard – muesli with prunes and figs and freshly brewed black coffee. As he ate his breakfast, he would skim the financial pages of the broadsheets.

After breakfast, his secretary would join him to take dictation. Sir Philip spurned emails and insisted that they were printed out so that he could deal with them along with the other correspondence in his in-tray (a real, not virtual, in-tray made of oak). This was typically old fashioned of Sir Philip. He stood aloof from technological developments. He also, it has to be said, often found it difficult to connect with younger members of staff. There was one famous occasion at a staff party when a young manager told Sir Philip that he used to work in the finance department at Ford Motor Company based in Dagenham. After a pause, Sir Philip, who had never been to Dagenham but knew it was beside the Thames, enquired in his usual courteous way, 'Good fishing in Dagenham?'

The rest of the day would be taken up with interminable meetings during which Sir Philip would behave impeccably. He would listen without interruption, paraphrase, make informative comments and never show any irritation come what may.

Sir Philip also spent a good deal of time mentoring the newly appointed managing director who exhibited some rough edges that Sir Philip was keen to smooth off. During his first few months, the MD had, on a number of occasions, been guilty of making off-the-cuff pronouncements that later had to be retracted. Sir Philip was determined to replace these impetuous tendencies with something more considered, where facts were weighed and pros and cons given careful deliberation. His calm temperament and orderly habits meant that he was admirably qualified to counsel the MD in such matters. The MD, however, was disappointingly stubborn and resistant to Sir Philip's persuasions. Despite this, Sir Philip kept at it like water dripping onto granite. His patience was legendary.

One day Sir Philip's secretary brought him a letter from a professor of psychology at a nearby university. The letter explained that the department had won a tender to conduct a preliminary enquiry into how top managers developed their skills and talents. In particular, the research would aim to identify the day-to-day experiences that provided the most useful opportunities for work-based learning. Sir Philip was sufficiently intrigued to offer himself as one of the guinea pigs.

A briefing meeting with the professor was arranged. Sir Philip was required to be shadowed by a young psychologist through three working days. The psychologist would keep a detailed log of all the activities that took place during his period of observation. This would be analysed and then, armed with this data, the professor would return to interview Sir Philip in order to discover which activities he had learned most from and to collect specific examples of his 'lessons learned'.

The shadowing passed with no snags. Sir Philip was co-operative and helpful throughout the three days and looked forward to hearing what emerged from the log and to the final interview with the professor.

After a couple of weeks, the good professor arrived for the session with Sir Philip. He had a printout listing 12 different activities in descending order based on the percentage of time they had consumed during the three days. Top of the list were the mentoring sessions with the MD, second was a lengthy meeting at the Treasury which had been chaired by the Chancellor in person, third was a board meeting and so on.

The professor congratulated Sir Philip on having such a rich and varied working life and started to probe gently for evidence of learning. Sir Philip was characteristically polite but was adamant that he himself had learned nothing from any of these experiences. When, for example, his mentoring sessions were explored, he could cite instances of learning by the MD, but was nonplussed at the suggestion that he too might have gained something from the encounters.

Try as he might, the professor always drew a blank. Sir Philip kept apologising for wasting the professor's time, but wouldn't budge from his position; he was there to help other people learn and develop, not to learn himself.

After many gallant attempts to extract some evidence of learning from Sir Philip, the professor eventually accepted defeat. As he left, Sir Philip shook him warmly by the hand and said, 'Most interesting. I must say that if you could make this learning business more respectable, maybe we could do something with it.'

Ah, thought the professor, so *that* was the problem: Sir Philip couldn't bring himself to admit to learning because it wasn't respectable.

Advice to Sir Philip

The more senior you are, the more the pressure is on you to seem wise and omnipotent. Being omnipotent and admitting to learning don't mix. I suspect, however, a more fundamental problem: you may well have taken the stance you did with the professor, not because you weren't learning, but because your learning was subliminal.

Let me explain. The majority of our everyday learning is informal. Something happens – it might or might not have been planned – and the experience generates some learning. However, precisely what we have learned is often vague and tacit rather than explicit. This is in contrast to formal learning where the whole process is more deliberate and conscious. At the end of a conference or course, for example, it is much easier to articulate some lessons learned than at the end of a busy day doing this and that. Since the professor was exploring your *informal* learning, the chances are that you hadn't got this together in an easily communicable form.

Your reticence with the professor may well have resulted from a combination of (a) having reservations about the wisdom of someone in your position admitting to learning and (b) the difficulties of articulating insights from your informal learning. Overcoming the latter would, I believe, help with the former.

All you need to do to 'surface' learning that would otherwise be subliminal and inaccessible is to ask yourself at, say, the beginning of a day or week, 'What did I learn yesterday/last week?' It is easier to answer this question if you focus your attention on one or two actual incidents and go back over them in your mind. Making a written note of your 'lessons learned' is a discipline that helps to crystallise your learning.

Once you are clear what you have learned, you are in a better position to decide whether or not to share it with other people. The choice is yours. There are two big advantages in sharing your learning with others. Firstly, you are being a role-model that others may emulate. This is admirable since learning is *the* core competence; the gateway to every other skill and capability people and organisations need. Secondly, people might learn from what you have learned. You may be offering them a ready-made insight that they can adapt and incorporate into their own *modus operandi*.

And just think, you could give the professor a call and rattle off some lessons learned! He'd be very impressed!

16
A manager who strove to give a student a really interesting week of work experience

Stephen was a successful businessman who ran his own publishing company. The publications were all of the pop psychology, self-help, 'you can do it if you really want to' genre. There were paperbacks about healthy eating, healthy exercising, healthy breathing, healthy relaxation, healthy sex and healthy brains. The books, though actually read by only 10 per cent of those who bought them, sold well and Stephen's company flourished.

As you might guess from the appearance of six 'healthys' in one sentence, Stephen was a man with a social conscience. It would be fair to describe him as a do-gooder. He believed passionately in spreading the word about healthy this and healthy that. He gave talks at local clubs and schools and put leaflets through letterboxes. He ran a website packed with articles about healthy living and a mini-Amazon facility so that customers could order his publications online.

Remarkably, he even practised what he preached. Each day he was careful to eat at least five portions of fruit and vegetables and drink three litres of water. He went for a brisk 30-minute walk each morning followed by 20 minutes of meditation. He took 1000 milligrams of fish-oil concentrate each morning with his muesli and did Pilates exercises to strengthen his body and improve his balance. Stephen came as close to being a paragon of virtue as mere mortals ever can.

One day Stephen went to an Education-Business Links Conference organised by Business in the Community. One of the speakers waxed lyrical about the need to forge stronger links between education and business. He urged every business to 'adopt' a local school and explore ways to help the staff and students understand, and better appreciate, the world of work. The speaker was adamant that, despite businesses being society's wealth creators, a career in business was often considered second best and that everyone should strive to improve work's image.

Stephen came away determined to play his part. He contacted the head teacher of his local comprehensive school and offered his services. The head teacher was surprised and suggested that Stephen come into the school a few times a week to hear some of the junior children reading. Stephen explained that, much as he would enjoy this, he had a business to run. Might there be some other way he could help that would not entail long absences from his desk? Yes, came the reply, how about offering work experience for sixth formers?

So it came to pass that a young lad, Graham, arrived one Monday morning, with a clipboard tucked under his arm. In the weeks leading up to this event Stephen had grown increasingly apprehensive. His staff made it clear that they thought this exercise largely a waste of time, another of Stephen's fads, and that they were not prepared to be burdened with a student asking them naïve questions all week. Stephen would have to take responsibility.

Stephen visited the government's website and, with sinking heart, read that students should benefit from work placements by:

- Experiencing and understanding the world of work.

- Applying knowledge and skills developed at school in a work-related context.

- Appreciating the relevance of education to the world of work.

- Developing skills, knowledge and confidence for adult life.

- Becoming more aware of rights and responsibilities in the workplace.

- Understanding employment opportunities and developing their personal career plans.

Daunting stuff. As the week approached, Stephen worried about how to give the student a sufficiently meaningful experience. He read and reread the briefing sheet that the school's careers teacher had provided and drew up a plan for the week that contained ample variety. It included an initial question- and-answer session about the company and its products, a short time with each member of the team finding out about their role, a couple of mini-projects which involved scrutinising the business plan and some of the company's marketing literature, shadowing Stephen on some customer visits and observing the weekly team meeting. The last 30 minutes of every day was to be spent looking back over the day's activities and writing up his learning log and each new day was to start with a discussion of the lessons he had learned the day before. And so on.

Once the plan had been drawn up, Stephen started to feel more confident. In fact, he felt positively virtuous! He was convinced he was about to provide a model week that would be an admirable advertisement for the much maligned world of work. Stephen decided to volunteer to take a student every year. His wife advised him not to make any sort of long-term commitment until he had survived the week.

As it turned out, Stephen found Graham hard work. He was very quiet and morose. Stephen spent the week meeting the boy more than half way. He longed for Graham to be livelier, and to show more enthusiasm for the company's wonderful publications, each of which, Stephen assured him, could literally transform someone's life. After work each evening, Stephen would feel quite drained. But next morning he would recover and devote his day to a demonstration of how fascinating and varied working in a small publishing company could be.

The week culminated with a final learning review and, as Stephen said goodbye and thanked Graham for all he'd done, he made a bad mistake. He asked Graham whether he'd found the week interesting. There was an ominous pause. 'No, not really' said Graham.

Advice to Stephen

I suspect that, in your anxiety to get things right, you erred on the side of over-structuring the week! You are clearly a conscientious person and I am aware that this comment must seem harsh in the face of all your efforts to give Graham a 'good experience'. I believe that, as far as Graham was concerned, the week with you seemed rather like an extension to his school timetable. Every moment was organised – just like a school that is fearful of building in any slack in case pupils couldn't cope or would get up to mischief.

I think a mix of activities, some structured by you and some where Graham had to take the initiative, would have given him a better understanding of work and, in particular, what it means to take responsibility for one's actions. Too many employees are spoon-fed to the extent that they become institutionalised and dependent – incapable of taking any initiatives without looking over their shoulders.

So, what could you have done differently?

I think you could have designed the week around a project. Think of a treasure hunt where participants have a series of clues, each posing a problem that they must solve in order to progress to the next clue. Suppose you had greeted Graham at the beginning of the week, briefed him on your expectations (see below), and then set him the task of finding out certain things about your publishing company. He could, for example, have been asked to pretend he was an outside consultant with a fresh pair of eyes and given the task of coming up with some ideas about what to do differently/better. You wouldn't necessarily expect great things; the whole point would be to provide him with a challenge. Instead of organising sessions with you and the staff, you could have asked him to draw up a list of questions, given him access to everyone, and let him interview the staff in search of answers. He could also have been let lose on the company's website and given things to read as background – the company's latest product catalogue, the business plan, marketing literature and other relevant documents. At the end of the week he could make a presentation to you and, if you felt he was up to it, to all the staff giving his impressions and recommendations.

Had you structured the week along these participative, 'its-up-to-you' lines, I very much doubt that Graham would have said the week with you was not interesting. Quite the contrary, he'd have probably said it was exhilarating and exhausting! Even if he thought the week hadn't been interesting, he'd have only had himself to blame.

When you brief new members of staff, and the Grahams of this world, it is a good idea to include something about your expectations (even better if you ask them to reciprocate and tell you their expectations!). If you are going to do this, you will need to work out what your expectations are. Just for starters, here are the ones I use – but you need to emulate this, not copy it. It is *your* expectations that count.

I always introduce this list by saying, 'Do these things and you'll exceed my expectations!'.

- If you aren't clear about something, always ask. Questions are welcome.

- If you are unhappy about something, always say so. Don't let things fester.

- If you see something that needs doing, just do it (it is easier to ask for forgiveness than for permission!).

- Experiment with different ways of doing things in order to find a way that works best.

- When you make a mistake (*when*, not *if!*), say sorry and learn from it.

- If you can see a way to improve something, go ahead and suggest it.

- If you aren't sure what other people think about your performance, ask for feedback.

- If something you have done is criticised, remember it is what you *did* that has attracted the criticism – *not* you as a person.

- Whenever possible, stay cheerful. It will help you to feel more positive – and it is nicer for your colleagues.

- Remember to use work as an opportunity to grow and develop your talents. Work isn't always fun, but if you keep learning even the bad times are worthwhile.

17

A manager who was hooked on initiatives

Brian was the managing director of a travel agency. He was in his mid-thirties, bursting with energy and keen to stamp his authority on the organisation. A sporting type, he had always been loud and enthusiastic. He was a big man, wore size 13 shoes (wide fitting), and had a flat nose that had received a battering in various boxing bouts and rugby matches. He also had a head of unruly blond hair that stuck out in all directions like a thatched roof after a storm.

Brian was determined to succeed. On his appointment, the chairman had set him the task of doubling turnover and profits within four years. Each morning, as he shaved in the mirror, Brian would psyche himself up to face the numerous challenges the day would bring. He made a point of arriving at work early, always ate lunch on the run and stayed late. It became a matter of pride that he was seen to work longer hours than anyone else. He frequently visited the high street branches to address the staff and boost their morale. Wherever he went, he explained the need for a step-change in order to meet the ambitious financial targets he had been set.

Within three months of his appointment, in a flurry of activity, Brian had launched a company-wide campaign called '4x2' – a title he thought of himself. Having launched the campaign, Brian knew that it was vital to maintain the momentum. He drew up lists of themes and initiatives and decided to launch them at the rate of one each month.

Some were designed to improve customer care, others to upgrade the IT system and other key processes, others to cut costs, others to enhance the company's image, others to achieve better marketing segmentation, others to switch to eLearning for staff training – and so on. Breathless stuff! Brian was definitely not short of initiatives.

Brian was an avid reader of management books and journals. He lapped up *The Harvard Business Review*, *Management Today*, books on leadership and managing change, quality management, and even learning organisations and emotional intelligence. He loved to keep abreast of the latest writings from the management gurus. Brian was what you might describe as an active reader. He always used a highlighter to mark passages in the text that took his fancy. He also kept a sheet of paper by his side and compiled an action list as he went along. These actions were added to his growing list of initiatives. Brian calculated that he had enough to last at least three years, by which time, he surmised, he would surely have been headhunted and moved on to new challenges.

After a year in the job, and initiatives galore, neither turnover nor profit showed any signs of improvement. Puzzled, Brian stepped up his efforts. He continued to launch new initiatives. He rushed around the country in a bid to re-galvanise people into action.

After another year of sweat and toil, turnover remained, stubbornly, much the same. Profits showed some modest improvement, but only because of some cost cutting – unprofitable branches had been closed and headcount had been reduced.

The chairman sent for Brian and announced that he no longer had the support of the board. His contract was to be terminated forthwith.

Advice to Brian

My commiserations – all your hard work failed to produce the required results. As I'm sure you appreciate, turnover and profit are dependent on many interrelated factors – some of them external to the company and beyond your control. It is quite possible that without your initiatives, the performance of the company would have declined. Looked at this way, keeping the turnover steady could be seen as a triumph! Pity that your chairman didn't see it this way.

I expect you are at the stage of licking your wounds and mulling over the experience? No doubt you can think of things you could have done differently and, knowing your love of action lists, I bet you have already identified some to carry forward into your next job.

I wonder whether you have 'initiatives' on your list? If not, I think you should have.

I suspect you are a fad surfer – an enthusiastic collector of the latest management theories. Fads, by definition, have a short shelf life. They tend to follow a pattern:

1. A book, written by a well-known guru, gets a high profile launch.

2. There is a lot of hype along the lines of 'This is *the* Answer.'

3. This is followed by a spate of conferences and articles in the management press saying 'You should try this.'

4. Some companies start to experiment with the approach.

5. The next book from the management guru production line is published.

6. People switch their attention to the new theory and the
    original one dips beneath the horizon.

There are two big lessons to learn from this iterative sequence of
events. First, despite rhetoric to the contrary, there are no
panaceas. Second, the attraction of the new, and the clamour for
instant answers, means that the band-wagon rolls on before
anything has had a chance to be tested.

With the benefit of hindsight, perhaps you can see how your
addiction to an unrelenting stream of initiatives closely follows the
same pattern. The trick is not to have lots of initiatives, but to be
highly selective and, above all, fastidious in following through the
few initiatives you implement.

If you keep launching initiatives people soon start suffering from
'initiative fatigue'. A sure sign of this is when people acquiesce but
drag their heels as they wait for the next flavour of the month to
emerge.

I imagine that many of your initiatives may have ineffectually fizzled
out because of a combination of cynicism ('Not another initiative!')
and fatigue.

The best antidote is to have a few, well-chosen, *sustainable*
initiatives that are vigorously tracked through to completion.

18

A head teacher who hardly ever put a foot wrong

Len was an experienced and successful head teacher of a large comprehensive school. He had a commanding presence – tall, slim, a fine head of greying hair and bright blue eyes. He was alive to every detail of his immediate surroundings. He moved quickly, spoke assertively and was always attentive and courteous. Whatever charisma is, he had it. Quite deservedly, he enjoyed the respect of his staff, the school governors, the pupils, the parents and the local community. He had consistently raised the standards in his school and received glowing Ofsted reports.

On closer analysis, Len had a number of enviable winning ways. For a start, he had a reputation for getting things done. It wasn't that he was necessarily an original thinker, more that he was open to new ideas, regardless of where they came from, and brilliant at implementing them. He exhibited the conviction of a true entrepreneur. Over the course of a number of years, he had succeeded in securing 25% of the school's total budget from external funding. This was achieved through a network of charitable trusts, limited companies and corporate sponsorship. He had, for example, negotiated a special deal with a computer manufacturer to supply laptops for each pupil in the sixth form. And the school was close to raising the funds to build a new sports centre.

Len's relations with the local community, and especially with employers in the school's catchment area, was second to none. He firmly believed that education was for life and made forging close and positive links with the world of work a priority. As a consequence, he had a cadre of business people he could call on for advice and guidance in such areas as finance, IT and marketing. His close relations with businesses also meant that pupils were offered a steady stream of worthwhile work-experience assignments.

Len liked to regard all his activities as experiments from which there was much to learn. He always had a number of things on the go – rather like a juggler keeping plates spinning on a long row of bamboo canes. He experimented with different ways to recruit staff and with different staff development methods. He experimented with a different timetable, with different teaching methods, with different menus at lunchtimes, with evening activities, with different ways to involve parents in the school's activities and with ways to treat everything that happened in the school as learning opportunities.

He resisted the temptation to micro-manage any of these projects. Instead he trusted his staff and gave them the space, authority and encouragement to experiment. Not all the experiments succeeded, of course, but that simply led to the identification of valuable lessons learned which were carried over into the next experiment.

Another remarkable thing about Len was that he could unhesitatingly put names to faces. No one could understand how he did it, but he only had to meet someone, hear their name once, and he'd got it. There were almost a thousand pupils in his school and he knew every one of them by name. When, each September, a new intake arrived, he'd have mastered their names within a couple of weeks. The same skill extended to parents and the many members of the local community he had dealings with.

Not only did he have many thousands of names and faces stored in his memory bank, but, somehow, he was able to retrieve the right name within a split second. Perhaps the most impressive example of this was when Len took part in various events organised by the school's alumni. Even after a couple of glasses of wine, he could remember the names of pupils who had left the school years before.

At an annual dinner to celebrate the school's 50th anniversary, Len was once again at his sparkling best. He circulated before dinner greeting people, as usual, by name. He made a funny speech recalling many of the significant moments in the school's recent history. He told a few anecdotes about some past members of staff and pupils who had been notably eccentric. But all the way through the meal he had been slightly distracted by someone sitting on a nearby table.

Len was distracted because, most unusually for him, he knew the young man's face but couldn't recall the name. Try as he might, the name eluded him. After dinner, Len decided to admit defeat and enlist the young man's help. Feeling rather foolish, Len said, 'I do apologise, your face is very familiar but I can't quite place you. Where have we met before?'

The young man laughed and said, 'Earlier this evening. We were in the gents together!'

Advice to Len

It sounds as if you have got everything going for you. Would that there were more head teachers of your calibre. All the research shows that the head's leadership is the single most important factor in determining the success of a school. I very much like the way you treat everything as an experiment. Life is just one experiment after another – all, of course, generating transferable learning.

I'm delighted to hear that you slip up occasionally! This gives you a chance to indulge in some self-deprecation. Confident people always poke fun at themselves; it provides the perfect antidote to coming across as arrogant and self-satisfied.

So, I strongly recommend that you add the story about the young man you had met but couldn't place, to your store of personal anecdotes. It shows that even paragons of virtue sometimes forget – and even go to the toilet occasionally!

19
A manager with Jekyll and Hyde characteristics

Roger was a senior manager in an advertising agency. He had a large team working for him – designers, graphic artists, copy writers as well as support people. His team were talented and creative and often won prestigious awards for their work.

Roger was a Jekyll-and-Hyde character. With outside clients, the media, anyone more senior and with certain favourites in his team, he was charming. He was highly articulate, with a deep voice, a quick sense of humour and an engaging smile. He was a large man, with photogenic facial features underneath a high forehead and a big bald head. When he was setting out to please, it was impossible to imagine that he could ever be anything other than delightful and charming. But in different circumstances a sinister Mr Hyde would appear.

If you weren't one of his favourites you ran the risk of being picked upon and victimised. This would take many forms. For example, Roger would select a piece of creative work, seemingly at random, and demolish it with criticism. He would threaten the unfortunate author with instant demotion unless they produced something better. Another of his ploys was to pick on a victim, give them a project to tackle and then browbeat them. Often this entailed phoning them at home at unreasonable times (usually early in the morning since Roger was an early riser) to demand an update. This would happen regardless of the agreed deadline for the project's completion.

However, by far the most trying aspect of Roger's darker side was the way he would pick on people during the regular team meetings he chaired. Hardly a week passed without someone in the team being singled out for special attention. It would start with a seemingly innocuous question about the progress of a given piece of work. Roger would find the answer inadequate and this would lead to another question, then another. The process would rapidly spiral into a full-scale public grilling and culminate in dire threats from Roger that things had better improve or else. Any defiance on the part of the victim merely prolonged the attack.

Over coffee one day, a number of the team were grumbling together about Roger's tyrannical behaviour. One of the newer members of the team, a young woman who had suffered a number of verbal assaults, said she thought she might have made an interesting discovery. She had noticed that when she sat opposite Roger at meetings, she was far more likely to be picked upon than if she sat alongside him. This observation led to an impromptu review of the correlation between seating positions in recent meetings and Roger's attacks. They decided it was a hypothesis worth testing.

The plan was for the people most often victimised by Roger to sit on his side of the table and for his favourites to sit opposite him. It was agreed to try this for an experimental four-week period and then to look at any trends that might have emerged.

To their surprise, it worked! Over the course of four meetings, members of the team tucked away in Roger's peripheral vision, never got picked on. Admittedly, some of his favourites, sitting opposite him as planned, did get picked on – but it was relatively mild, half-hearted stuff. Roger definitely soft-pedalled with his favourites. Armed with this insight, the team agreed a seating plan to ensure that Roger's favourites always took the chairs on the opposite side of the table. Fortunately, this was easy to accomplish since Roger never varied his seating position – dead centre on one side of a rectangular table.

One day the agency's personnel manager joined the meeting to brief Roger and his team on plans to refurbish their floor of the building. In passing, he suggested they might prefer a round table in the proposed new meeting room. To his surprise, this met with fierce resistance. For reasons he couldn't fathom, everyone seemed immoderately attached to the long rectangular table!

Advice to Roger

You are clearly anxious to improve the performance of some members of your team. At present you are attempting to accomplish this by turning up the heat. But ask yourself – is it working? When you apply pressure by harrying people and criticising their work, does it make a difference? Are there discernible signs of improvement?

Clearly, you have a vested interest in saying yes to these questions! But have you any hard evidence to substantiate your claim?

I suggest you try an experiment. Take two under-performing members of your team – let's call them A and B. Give them both a piece of work to be submitted to you by an agreed date. Pressurise person A by constantly chasing them and criticising their work. Insist that they improve the work in the light of your criticisms. By contrast, leave person B to get on with it and, when they produce the work, praise some good aspects and invite them to suggest ways it could be made even better.

If they are normal human beings, person A will be resentful and will only do the minimum to get it past you. Person B on the other hand, will show more enthusiasm and be keener to make improvements.

Now switch your tactics so that A gets the praise and B the criticism. Do their reactions change and, more importantly, does A's work improve and B's decline?

Hopefully this experiment will demonstrate that if you want to improve people's performance, coaching them in a supportive way will produce better results than being critical and heavy handed.

The 'if' in the last sentence is, however, an important proviso. I am assuming, perhaps naïvely, that the reason why you single out some members of your team, is because they are the ones you have decided are under-performing and require extra attention. This assumption gives you the benefit of the doubt. If in fact you have other motives, such as getting some sort of perverse pleasure out of belittling people in public, then this amounts to unacceptable harassment and I hope that sooner or later someone takes you to court.

The whole point of being a manager is to develop people's capabilities so that they perform well. It is a win-win. You get a motivated team who can be relied on to produce the goods and your staff get to improve their talents and become more marketable.

20

A manager who was a know-all and went to great lengths to win every argument

Keith was the managing director of a construction company. A qualified surveyor, he had long since abandoned his profession as he rose, too rapidly for his own good, through the management hierarchy.

Keith had some very irritating characteristics. First, he always, even when angry, wore a supercilious smile. It was an 'I'm better than you' smile. Second, he didn't walk; he strutted and, thirdly, he *always* knew best.

Whatever the topic or occasion, Keith behaved as if he knew more than anyone else who might be present. When, for example, he met a neuroscientist at a party, he knew more about synapses, plasticity and the workings of the brain. Once, watching his young son play in a prep-school cricket match, he found himself sharing a bench with the Foreign Secretary (whose son happened to be playing in the visiting team). Keith behaved as if he knew much more about world affairs and foreign policy than the minister. It was the same when he had a chance encounter with the Archbishop of Canterbury during the interval at a promenade concert in the Albert Hall. Suddenly he was an authority on God, falling church attendances, female bishops and homosexuality among the priesthood.

Needless to say these know-all tendencies extended to Keith's interactions at work. He *always* knew more about absolutely everything – the newest building methods and materials, the effect of strong winds on tall buildings, health and safety regulations, the stock market – his knowledge was apparently boundless.

Keith's unrelenting arrogance affected people in different ways. Some, who would normally be talkative, even a touch boastful, would lapse into a submissive silence. Others would initially be indignant, and for a while attempt to match Keith point by point, only to give up once they realised the futility of getting Keith to back down or admit that he didn't know what he was talking about. Yet others would be so incensed that they'd summon up hidden reserves and, astonishing even themselves, become fiercely competitive, determined to win the day. Other people, very sensibly, reacted to Keith by doing their best to ignore him and carry on with their lives.

One of the consequences of Keith's arrogance was that he had, simply *had*, to win every argument. When he went to a meeting (and that was often!) he would seize on some small point and prolong the discussion until he had prevailed. Any resistance was counter-productive; it simply extended the debate. If someone was unwise enough to produce a slipshod argument, Keith would swoop on it and persist until the unfortunate person had been beaten into submission. If there were no contentious points, then Keith would invent some.

One day Keith had an important meeting to chair in the boardroom. The meeting, scheduled to start at 10.30 am with clients from Malaysia, had been arranged to finalise a contract worth millions of pounds. Naturally Keith had prepared for the meeting by going through the draft contract line by line. At 10.00 am, with everything ready, Keith visited the toilet and was outraged to find that it hadn't been cleaned and that two of the lavatory bowls were blocked. He burst into the nearest office and demanded that the astonished occupants call up maintenance and ask someone to come and fix the toilets as a matter of extreme urgency.

Keith considered it so important to have the toilets in order before his important visitors arrived that he decided to wait and personally check that the necessary actions were under way. An apologetic maintenance manager was soon on the scene, with a janitor in tow, puzzled about why the toilets hadn't been serviced in the usual way.

As they set to work on the blockages Keith said, sarcastically, 'Thomas Crapper would be proud of you.' The maintenance manager replied 'Surely you mean Thomas Twyford?' 'No,' snapped Keith, 'I mean Thomas Crapper, the inventor of the water closet.'

If the conversation had ended there, all would have been well. Unfortunately the maintenance manager, not appreciating the folly of his action, stood his ground and said, 'I happen to know that it was Thomas Twyford who invented the first trapless china water closet in 1885.'

'Oh, come, come,' replied Keith dismissively, '*Everyone* knows that the water closet was invented by Thomas Crapper in the mid-1800s.'

'Well,' said the maintenance manager, 'I'm pretty sure you'll find that, despite rumours to the contrary, Crapper was a successful plumber but he did *not* invent the water closet.'

For Keith this was the equivalent of a red rag to a bull. He rushed back into the next door office, commandeered the nearest computer and typed 'inventor of the water closet' into the Google search engine. There he learnt that the earliest water closet was invented by Sir John Harrington in 1596 and was reinvented two hundred years later by

Alexander Cummings. However, Thomas Twyford emerged as the master toilet maker in, damn it, 1885. It was a myth that toilets were invented by Thomas Crapper.

Mortified at being found wrong, Keith printed off the information and rushed to the boardroom still clutching the data from PlumbingWorld.com. His contretemps with the maintenance manager meant that he was 15 minutes late and his Malaysian guests were not amused.

In the circumstances, the excuse that he had been delayed arguing about who had invented the water closet seemed inadequate to the occasion.

Advice to Keith

It sounds as if you need to sort out your priorities. Learning about the history of the water closet, fascinating though it is, could have waited until after your important meeting. Your compulsion to win every argument, however trivial, needlessly prolongs meetings and causes widespread resentment amongst your colleagues.

It is tempting to ask why you need to prove yourself more knowledgeable than anyone else you encounter, but I think it might be more productive to focus on *when* rather than *why*. Answers to *why* would undoubtedly lead to a fascinating psychoanalysis. But increased self-awareness does not necessarily result in behaviour change. Quite the contrary, it often provides a handy excuse to carry on exactly as before ('I can't help it. It's the way I was potty trained!'). So, let's skip the *whys* and concentrate on the *whens*.

There will be times when to indulge in some intellectual point scoring will be the equivalent of harmless fun. You clearly relish blowing your own trumpet and 'winning' probably gives you immense pleasure, rather like successfully mastering a difficult crossword or su doku. There are clearly other times when your compulsion to win gets in the way of achieving far more important things.

I suggest you work out when it is okay to indulge yourself and when to resist the temptation. If you can bring yourself to make the right choices, not only will this mean that important occasions will no longer be put in jeopardy, paradoxically it will also make your game playing *more* satisfying, not less. This is because intermittent reinforcement, i.e. sometimes winning, but not always, is far more thrilling than winning every single time. People are attracted to gambling precisely because winning is intermittent. If winning was guaranteed, no one would ever become addicted and gambling would be impossible!

Your victories will be far, far sweeter if you exercise choice. All you need to do is identify those occasions when point scoring is inappropriate. Examples might be:

- When there are bigger prizes to be won – your meeting with the representatives from Malaysia is a classic example.

- When it is important to bolster someone else's confidence rather than risk undermining it by showing you know best.

- When you are under tight time constraints and cannot afford to prolong things.

- When you are in listening mode, wanting to discover other people's perspectives and points of view, e.g. when interviewing.

- When you are with colleagues who are already in awe of your knowledge, i.e. you have nothing to prove.

A few criteria such as these should do the trick. You probably only need three or four and they will be easier to remember than a long, prohibitive list. When your criteria do not apply, you can give yourself permission to indulge in some showing off, confident that the consequences will not be too dire.

21

A manager who lacked social skills

Fred was the managing director of a large software company. He cut an unlikely figure – entirely bald, enormously fat, with tie askew and an unbuttoned jacket revealing a pair of wide braces holding up his trousers. He was also extraordinarily uncouth, peppering his sentences with expletives regardless of his audience. By no stretch of the imagination could Fred be said to be politically correct or to display any sensitivity or interpersonal skills.

But the man had a brilliant mathematical brain. In the evenings he would wander into a nearby office and challenge anyone there to a game of bridge or chess – for high stakes, naturally. His prowess at these games was legendary. He never lost. Of course, it is possible that he always triumphed because his victims feared that beating Fred might be career-limiting!

One day at a board meeting it was decided to establish a management training unit. Fred was party to the decision even though he himself was self-taught, knew nothing about training and didn't hold it in high regard. He merely shrugged his vast shoulders and let it through on the nod. There was surplus money in the budget and if a consensus of his directors wanted it, then what the hell? The company had never had any sort of systematic approach to management training before. They occasionally sent managers to outside courses, but this was done in a haphazard way, and no one ever bothered to evaluate the results.

An area sales manager, Hugh, was appointed to set up the unit. He too, had few ideas on how to go about this, so he engaged a consultant to help him establish a strategy and recruit some trainers. Since they were starting from scratch, the consultant recommended that each of the directors should be interviewed to gather their ideas on priorities for the proposed unit.

A structure for the interviews was agreed. Hugh would give the opening *spiel* and then hand over to the consultant to ask the questions. The first question was to be: 'Now that there is to be a management training unit, what difference would you like it to make?' The consultant told Hugh that this was a splendid open-ended question that would start the directors talking. All they had to do was put the question, listen hard, make notes on the directors' answers and, perhaps, ask a few supplementary questions. The directors were to be interviewed one by one, with Fred saved until last.

The interviews went according to plan. Everyone had sensible comments to offer in response to the open-ended question and Hugh and the consultant were able to draw up a preliminary list of priorities for the proposed management training unit. Then it was time to interview Fred and put the finishing touches to the plans.

The consultant hadn't met Fred before but had already heard company gossip about his unconventional appearance and ways. An appointment was made for the interview to take place at head office – a grand Georgian building in central London. Hugh was understandably nervous and it didn't help that they were made to wait in an anteroom before being ushered into Fred's presence.

There he sat, looking remarkably like a Chinese fertility god, behind a vast desk covered in papers. Alarmingly, his eyes were shut and he made no attempt to meet and greet. Hugh gave his usual *spiel* – faster than he had before. Fred sat, eyes shut. No nods, no anything. Then, undaunted, the consultant asked the pre-arranged question. 'Now that there is to be a management training unit, what difference would you like it to make?'

Nothing happened. The eyes stayed firmly shut. Hugh prodded the consultant (it would have been better if he had prodded Fred!) urging him to say something else. But the consultant felt stubborn. The question had worked well with half a dozen directors, why shouldn't it work on Fred? What was so special about this man?

Eventually Fred opened his eyes and spoke. He said, 'I wish my fucking managers would spend the company's fucking money as if it was their fucking own.'

His eyes then closed again, and that was that.

Advice to Fred

You are clearly a brilliant man who enjoys being an eccentric. Some of your unconventional ways are harmless and, no doubt, add light relief in what is often a drab, uninspiring commercial world. Eccentricities are welcome provided they do not have a detrimental effect on people's performance.

Your role as managing director is to do all you can to create an environment at work where people are productive and developed. Unfortunately, whether you like it or not, you are a key player in creating a productive work culture. People in organisations are particularly sensitive to everything senior managers say and do (particularly do!). You can be quite sure that gossip about some of your unusual characteristics is rife within your organisation. You can also be sure that if you, for example, are rude and uncouth, these behaviours will be imitated by others as a way of seeking your approval. You may think this pathetic – but that's the way it is. You are a trend-setter.

So, I recommend that you sort your eccentricities into those that are harmless and those that are likely to undermine people's performance. All you have to do is ask yourself, 'When I do this, is it likely to help or hinder other people's performance?'

You could try this on a whole host of things you tend to do. I suggest you start with the following:

- Being insensitive to other people's feelings.

- Being inept at interpersonal skills.

- Challenging people to play bridge/chess with you.

- Letting boardroom decisions with cost implications go by 'on the nod'.

- Keeping visitors waiting in your anteroom.

- Having your eyes shut.

- Failing to greet visitors to your office.

- Not acknowledging Hugh's introduction.

- Using the F word (three times in a single sentence!).

You'll probably conclude that some of these things are relatively harmless (for example, playing bridge/chess with staff in the evenings) whilst conceding that other things have an adverse effect (for example, failing to meet and greet visitors to your office). I certainly hope you will see that, to take just one example, failing to put Hugh and the consultant at ease when they kept their appointment with you, resulted in a less productive exchange of views than if you had greeted them in a more conventional way.

The decision, as ever, is yours – but never doubt that your behaviour has an impact, for better or worse.

22
A manager who became the victim of unintended consequences

Larry was the owner-manager of a very successful laundry. It specialised in hotel and restaurant linen. Every day, including weekends, a fleet of vans set off on their respective rounds delivering large wicker baskets of clean linen and collecting the dirty linen. On the whole the drivers had good, friendly relationships with the staff they dealt with at the various hotels and restaurants. The drivers would frequently stop to enjoy a chat over a cup of tea and a cigarette.

Larry couldn't believe his luck. He had bought the laundry as an ailing business five years previously and had worked hard to build it up into a profitable operation. He had invested in new equipment and engaged a marketing agency to promote the laundry's services. In fact, Larry was quite an entrepreneur. He had left school at 16 with no worthwhile qualifications and worked in a variety of dead-end jobs. He had joined the laundry as a foreman and watched it go into decline as the owner became increasingly frail and dispirited after a stroke. Larry took the initiative and struck an advantageous deal with the owner – a sort of tapered management buyout – who retired but remained a significant shareholder.

Having rescued the laundry and put it on a sure footing, Larry made a serious mistake. The van drivers were unionised and during protracted negotiations Larry agreed to a 'finish and go' scheme in return for no increase in wages. At the time this seemed like a good idea. It was popular with the men (to whom it gave an opportunity to obtain second jobs) and it limited overheads at the laundry. The alternative had been to agree to a generous wage increase.

After the new arrangement had been put in place, all went well for a few weeks. Or rather it didn't, but it was too early for Larry to notice. The first signs of a problem were when the assistant manager from one of the laundry's best customers, a prestigious hotel, telephoned Larry to complain that the driver had been rude to the housekeeper. Apparently, the driver arrived early and the laundry for collection hadn't been ready. Instead of sitting down for his usual chat, the driver had been abusive and a full-blown row had ensued.

This was the start of an alarming trend as similar complaints about the drivers' rudeness began arriving in Larry's office.

As if this wasn't enough, another consequence of the 'finish and go' arrangement gradually became evident. The vehicle accident rate went up. Nothing too serious, just minor knocks and scrapes, but the repair bill from the garage that maintained the fleet of vehicles rapidly doubled, then tripled.

The magnitude of his mistake slowly dawned on Larry. As the complaints poured in, and as some lucrative contracts were cancelled, he realised for the first time that his drivers were the laundry's ambassadors. They were the key point of contact with his customers and the relationship between them was vital to the success of the business. The 'finish and go' scheme was jeopardising a critical relationship with those who mattered most – the laundry's customers.

Larry opened negotiations with the van drivers' union in a desperate bid to reverse the mistake. A wise union rep, over a beer one evening, told Larry that he was the victim of unintended consequences.

'Seen it all before', he said. 'The trick is to ask yourself "in how many ways could this go wrong?" *before* you take action. Bloody sight better than finding out afterwards.'

Advice to Larry

I realise I'm rubbing salt into your wounds, but I'm afraid the union rep is right!

Every action generates a series of consequences in rather the same way a pebble thrown into a pond causes ripples. Furthermore, each consequence generates another consequence and so on in a never-ending sequence. Not surprisingly, therefore, unintended consequences have a nasty habit of creeping into the sequence when you least expect them. History is full of mishaps brought about by unintended consequences.

The answer is to accept that your actions will *always* have knock-on effects. If this wasn't the case there would be no point in implementing them. Consequences follow actions as night follows day. Some of the consequences will be expected and some will be unexpected, some welcome and some unwelcome.

The only way to prevent yourself falling victim to unintended consequences is, before implementing a major action, to discipline yourself to pause and think about the possible consequences. Divide a sheet of paper into two columns, the left-hand column for 'nice' consequences and the other for 'nasty' consequences. Work particularly hard at identifying possible nasty consequences. Involve some colleagues so that you gather different perspectives and points of view. They may well alert you to things that wouldn't have occurred to you.

When you and/or your colleagues have thought this through, estimate the likelihood of each consequence actually occurring. Use a simple rating system such as 1 for very likely to 5 for very unlikely.

If you have identified any nasty consequences that you have rated as likely (i.e. with ratings of 1, 2 or 3), this should set the alarm bells ringing and cause you to think again about the wisdom of proceeding.

I'm afraid there is no guaranteed way to protect yourself from all unintended consequences, but deliberately setting out to anticipate them will at least reduce your exposure.

23
A manager who failed to walk his talk

Mark was the managing director of a software house that administered the payrolls of a number of blue-chip companies. He was a chartered accountant and impressively computer-literate. He didn't particularly *look* like an accountant, however – more like a university professor. He had a beard, reading spectacles hung on a cord round his neck, and he was given to wearing cardigans with leather patches on both elbows. On hot days he discarded shoes and socks (and the cardigan!) in favour of a pair of battered leather sandals. He was a keen cyclist and had a fold-up bicycle that he carried on to the train each day so that at Paddington station he could erect it and pedal the last two miles into work.

Mark gave the impression of being a straightforward type. He was a lay preacher at his local church and was particularly interested in ethics. A year or so before, Mark had convened a number of meetings where a code of ethics for the business was hammered out. Having consulted widely, Mark personally drew up a written policy that set out standards and guidelines for ethical behaviour. Mark seized every opportunity to promote the idea of integrity as the best foundation for a good, sustainable business.

Mark didn't just 'preach' ethics. He fully understood the importance of being a role-model by walking the talk and backing up his words with actions. He consciously behaved in ways that demonstrated his own high standards. For example, he always gave honest answers to questions from staff, suppliers and customers. On the rare occasions when some item was confidential or sensitive, he'd say so and promise a full explanation as soon as it was possible to give one. He did his utmost to foster open communications, believing it was better to err on the side of providing people with too much information rather than too little. He encouraged staff to consult him whenever they had an ethical dilemma and frequently referred to the written guidelines to resolve issues.

So far so good. Besides being a keen cyclist, Mark was also a sailor. He owned a 20-foot yacht that he kept in a marina in the Portsmouth area. His wife, though, didn't share his passion for sailing. When they were first married, she had dutifully accompanied Mark, but she easily became seasick and invariably found the experience cold and uncomfortable. When she became pregnant with their first child, she used it as an excuse to stay at home and subsequent children made this a permanent arrangement. Over the years they had established a compromise whereby Mark went sailing one weekend each month, weather permitting, and for two weeks in the summer when he ventured further afield.

One year Mark set off on his customary two-week vacation, sailing across the channel and along the French coast to the Channel Islands. He telephoned his wife a couple of times to say all was well but didn't come home in time to return to work on the Monday. Mark's wife phoned the office to say he was not back yet and by Wednesday had informed the police that he was missing.

A week later, the coastguard found the wreckage of Mark's yacht on some rocks in Cornwall. The wreckage showed there had been a fire at sea. There was no sign of Mark.

After another week, Mark's partially decomposed body was washed up on a beach 20 miles further along the coast. Dental records helped to confirm his identity. His wife and children were understandably distraught.

Two weeks later another body was found on the same stretch of seashore. The body was female and there were clear signs that it had suffered extensive burning. Over the ensuing weeks it slowly became clear that Mark had been having an extra-marital affair. For the past three years the mystery woman had been his willing sailing companion.

What happened on that final journey was never fully established. Everyone who had known Mark was incredulous to discover that their high-principled role model had been deceiving his wife.

Advice to Mark

Alas, I am too late to offer you any advice because you are dead.

I find it extraordinary that you could lead a double life, apparently for a number of years, so successfully. This is quite an accomplishment. Most managers would find it a challenge to sustain a whopping lie so convincingly.

What, however, would I have recommended *if* I had caught up with you before your sad demise? This is assuming you'd have felt able to confide in me – unlikely, I think, having apparently perfected your double life.

First, I'd have urged you to think through the consequences of being discovered; the effect it would have on your colleagues at work and, of course, on your wife and family. The emphasis you placed on openness and honesty, would certainly have left you exposed as a hypocrite and it was totally predictable that your wife and children would be devastated. Trust in you would have been shattered.

Having encouraged you to reflect on this, I would have urged you to decide what to do to retrieve the situation. Basically you had four options:

1. To do nothing.

2. To discontinue your extra-marital affair.

3. To leave your wife.

4. To confess to your wife.

We would have explored each of these options, and others you may have thought of, working out the pros and cons of each. I would have facilitated this process, letting your preferred course of action emerge during the course of our discussion. Whatever the outcome, I would have respected your confidences and offered you support.

What a shame you let it all go pear-shaped and caused such widespread distress.

24

A manager who loved to wander around

There was a very senior HR manager whose name was Albert. He, as you might guess both from his name and from the fact that he was very senior, was nearing a comfortable retirement and, so far as anyone could tell, did little actual work. He was, however, very good at wandering around.

Quite possibly, but this is sheer speculation, he had read an article by Tom Peters about the perils of senior managers losing touch and had latched on to the idea of Management by Wandering Around as a practical solution.

Whatever the reason, Albert spent a good part of his day simply wandering around, beaming at people and asking them how they were. Despite (or perhaps because of) his seniority, he did this in a very genial way. He also looked the part, with a cheerful round face, abnormally bushy, expressive eyebrows and half-spectacles that slid down his nose. He always wore a bow tie.

The few words he exchanged with the hapless staff he happened to encounter on his random wanderings followed a distinct pattern. It went like this:

'Ah, um, good to see you. How are you?'

'Fine, thank you, Mr Albert.'

'Jolly good, jolly good.'

Now there are a number of points to notice about this exchange.

First, Albert was infamous for never remembering anyone's name, so he simply called everyone he met Um. No one could remember Albert ever addressing anyone by name. Rumour had it that he even called his nearest and dearest Um.

Second, it was a longstanding tradition to call Albert 'Mr Albert'. Now this might strike you as old-fashioned and completely out of kilter with the modern habit of calling everyone, even complete strangers, by their first name. But that was the way it was.

Third, you might think the retort 'Jolly good, jolly good' to be unremarkable when someone has just told you they are fine. But would you think it appropriate if someone had just told you they felt ill, or were stressed out, or were going on strike, or had an insoluble problem to solve by an impossible deadline?

The trouble with Albert was that he never varied his patter. He produced 'how are yous' and 'jolly goods' as an automatic reflex.

One day the exchange went like this:

'Ah, um, good to see you. How are you?'

'Well, Mr Albert, I'm sorry to say that my wife is in intensive care and I ran over the cat this morning.'

'Jolly good, jolly good.'

Advice to Albert

It is good that you are getting out of your office and making yourself visible. Too many managers busy themselves managing the other resources (for example, bricks and mortar, finances and equipment) and pay insufficient attention to the most important resource of all – their people.

However, you clearly need to brush up your technique! You need to vary your patter and, most important of all, you need to ask questions and listen like hell to the answers. The whole point of management by wandering around is to have meaningful interactions, not sterile, ritualistic exchanges. You need to learn how to ask questions that are likely to elicit worthwhile answers.

At present you aren't a) asking any questions that are likely to stimulate interesting answers and b) listening. Even if, by some fluke, you got a good answer, the chances are that it would pass you by and you'd give it the 'jolly good' treatment.

What sort of questions could you usefully ask as you do your wandering? Try some like these:

- What are you working on at the moment?

- What is the biggest work problem facing you right now?

- If you had a magic wand and could wave it over this place, what would you change?

- What do you want managers to do more of? Less of?

- What would we need to change to make you even more effective?

- What is the most interesting thing that has happened to you this past week – and what have you learned from it?

- What extra help or support would you like? How can I help you?

All these questions are thought-provoking and none of them can be answered with a straightforward yes or no. Don't necessarily expect to get good answers straight way. People will need a period of adjustment – to get over the shock of being listened to! When you ask a decent question and fail to get a satisfactory answer, suggest that they sleep on it and give you their answer in the morning (and make a note to follow them up if they don't volunteer one).

Oh, and for goodness sake, make it your business to learn some names!

25

A manager who couldn't resist relying on his predecessor's advice

Simon had worked all his life in business and commerce and the time had come, as it must, to retire. His career had been one of unblemished success. He had been knighted three years previously for services to industry. He served on a variety of government advisory boards and had the ear of the Chancellor and the Prime Minister. Besides being chairman of an international financial institution, he held an impressive string of directorships. His opinions on current events were frequently sought and, from time to time, he was interviewed on radio and television.

Simon even looked the part. He had Cary Grant features – tall, square-jawed, with a fine head of white hair. Clear blue eyes looked out confidently over half-spectacles. He always wore dark Armani pin-striped suits, complemented by sober ties and immaculate shirts.

The numerous colleagues who worked with Simon in various capacities found him wise and genuinely helpful. People would seek him out to ask his advice on weighty matters and for many years he had mentored a number of less experienced managers, all of whom had flourished under his patronage.

Simon was steadfast in concentrating on four themes:

• Fostering visionary champions of change.

123

- Unlocking people's potential.

- Knowing and exceeding customer expectations.

- Introducing new, differentiated products and services.

He was adamant that research had shown time and time again that nine out of ten successful businesses were successful precisely because they did these four things better, and more consistently, than their competitors.

Simon, besides remaining focused, was also remarkable in displaying a positive attitude come what may. No one ever caught him being fractious or despondent. He carried a piece of paper tucked inside his pocket diary and sometimes he'd fish it out and show it to one of his mentees. It said:

What is, not what isn't.
What can, not what can't.
What will, not what won't.
What does, not what doesn't.
What has, not what hasn't.

Characteristically, Simon looked forward to his impending retirement with enormous enthusiasm. He had compiled a list of activities he was keen to undertake; go to more concerts and opera, write a book encapsulating his management philosophy; read more biographies, walk the Ridgeway, the Pembrokeshire coastal path, explore the Scottish Highlands. He also planned to give up some of his directorships and adopt a charity – preferably one promoting educational opportunities for the under-privileged and those who had been alienated by their compulsory education.

As expected, Simon's deputy, Henry, was duly selected to be his successor – a man he had brought on through coaching and mentoring. During the three-month hand-over period they worked closely together.

On Simon's last day, before the sumptuous celebration lunch that had been planned, Simon drew Henry aside. He explained that he had written three messages giving helpful advice in the event of a crisis. The messages were numbered and locked in a tin box (the sort you'd keep petty cash in). In no circumstances were they to be opened except in the event of a crisis. Henry thanked Simon and took the key to the box.

Six months later a new computer system was installed. Specifying and developing it had cost a vast amount of money but it quickly became clear that there were appalling problems which threatened the stability of the entire business. The suppliers made reassuring noises and said that the problems could be overcome if a dedicated team worked on them non-stop for a few weeks – or it might be months.

Henry decided that this was a crisis. He opened the tin box and took out Simon's first envelope. He opened it and read the advice. It simply said: *If I were you, I'd go back to square one.* Henry sacked the suppliers, found new ones and started all over again.

After another six months a serious dispute with the unions erupted. Negotiations broke down and the unions, confident that they had a strong case, announced that they were going to ballot their members and recommend strike action. If this happened it would be the first strike in the company's history and be severely damaging.

Henry decided that this was another crisis, opened the tin box and took out Simon's second envelope. He opened it and read the advice. It said: *If I were you, I'd go to arbitration.* Henry suggested to the union representatives that the best course of action was to take the dispute to the arbitration service and agree to abide by their decision. This led to a satisfactory resolution and a strike was averted.

After a further six months the company suffered two simultaneous set-backs. First, it was successfully attacked by internet fraudsters who, over a matter of days, spirited large amounts of money away overseas. Second, a rogue trader incurred such serious losses that the continued existence of the organisation was in jeopardy.

Henry was in no doubt that this was a crisis and he opened the tin box and took out Simon's third envelope. He opened it and read Simon's advice. It said: *If I were you, I'd start writing your three messages.*

Advice to Henry

Clearly I am not best qualified to say this, but I think you should wean yourself off Simon's advice! Throw away that silly tin box and make your own decisions.

Advice of the 'if I were you' variety is always suspect and should be treated with the utmost caution. Simon was clearly an impressive bloke, and no doubt you learnt a great deal from him during the hand-over period, but he has gone now and you are running the show.

I think there is a difference between being given unsolicited advice and actively seeking it. By all means seek advice from other people in order to add it to your list of options or to seek reassurance that you are not alone in deciding on a particular course of action. Clearly, there is much to learn from comparing your perceptions and conclusions with those of other people. It would be foolish not to benefit from being exposed to diverse views.

Of course, what matters in the end is the extent to which advice from other people helps you to make a better decision than you would have made without it. You can check on this by reaching your own conclusion first, then seeking advice and seeing how often it causes you to modify your initial opinion.

Using advice to add value to your decisions is wise. Being dependent on advice is feeble.

Part 2:
Stories about middle and junior managers

See Chapter 31

26

A manager who insisted words could only be used if precise definitions had been agreed

Nick was a human relations manager in a large telecommunications business. He had many years' experience of HR, having worked in a diverse range of industries from car manufacture to food processing to computers.

Nick a man of average build who looked remarkably like 1960s prime minister Harold Wilson without the pipe. He was fond of pontificating and could produce an instant opinion on, well, anything! Over the years, Nick had formed strong views about many issues, particularly about the role of HR and the many dilemmas it faced as a service activity. He was prone to launch into homilies on what the HR function should do and should not do for line managers. His general view was that line managers were poor at managing people and that HR had to work hard to compensate. However, he was clear that it would be a mistake for HR to let line managers escape their responsibilities. He maintained that it was a matter of working out what to do *for* the line and what to do *with* the line. He was adamant that HR should be an active participant in all major business decisions, but that a place at the top table had to be earned rather than expected.

Many years previously Nick had come across Transactional Analysis and it still exerted a strong influence over the way he saw the world. He was fond of labelling people according to what he imagined was their predominant ego state. He'd come away from a difficult meeting with a line manager muttering about crossed transactions and having been on the receiving end of too much 'critical parent'. Or, if someone was flippant, he'd put it down to a surfeit of 'natural child'. Sometimes – not often – he would claim that an interaction, even with a line manager, had been 'adult to adult'.

He was fond, too, of identifying the psychological 'games' people played at work. He would often confront someone by saying, 'Ah, you're playing "Yes But" with me!' or, 'That's the "I Was Only Trying To Help" game.' When Nick exposed what he asserted was a game, he would do so with unrestrained relish. Anyone who had the audacity to question his prognosis was accused of playing the innocent victim and resorting to the 'Who, Me?' game.

Not content with the games described in Eric Berne's book *Games People Play*, Nick would invent games to fit the situation. If, for example, someone grumbled about a colleague, they'd be accused of playing the 'It's All Their Fault' game. If someone capitulated too easily, they'd be accused of playing 'Anything For A Quiet Life'. If someone in a meeting suggested that more data should be collected before a decision could be made, they'd be accused of playing the 'Analysis to Paralysis' game. If, on the other hand, someone made an instant decision, they'd be accused of playing the 'Quick Fix' game. Whatever happened, Nick was ready with a game to fit the circumstances.

For Nick, the one basic message was the need for authentic communication between consenting adults. He maintained that the onus was *always* on the communicator, and that if the receiver of a communication was unclear or confused then the transmitter of the communication was responsible, not the receiver. From time to time,

Nick would drive the message home by insisting that the receiver of a message described, in their own words, the meaning they had derived. Nick would then turn to the communicator and ask whether that was an accurate interpretation. Whenever it wasn't, Nick would beam happily, like a schoolteacher catching someone misbehaving behind the bicycle sheds.

The MD of the company decided to take a number of the most senior directors away to a hotel for a couple of days where they would spend time working on a ten-year strategy for the business. Nick, even though he wasn't a member of the MD's inner cabinet, was invited to join them. He was delighted to receive the invitation, which he considered a long overdue vote of confidence in the HR function. He saw it as a rare opportunity to demonstrate the added value that HR could contribute.

The meeting began, and it wasn't long before Nick realised that some words were being banded about with no agreed understanding of their meaning. The word 'strategy' was one example. So far as Nick could make out, to some people this appeared to mean a vision, to others an objective, to others a plan and so on. Nick toyed with the idea of intervening but decided to bide his time and see how the conversation developed.

Other words were used, such as 'paradigm' and 'differentiation', and Nick became increasingly concerned that there was no shared understanding. Eventually, he could bear it no longer. He leaped up, rushed to the flip chart, snatched up a felt-tipped pen and wrote the word STRATEGY in big capital letters.

'Gentlemen,' said Nick, 'You ought to agree what this word means! A shared understanding is absolutely essential before you move on.'

The MD replied, 'Thank you Nick, but I don't think that will be necessary.'

'But,' said Nick, determined to seize the moment, 'There are a number of different meanings in this room and unless you bottom them out you'll be hampered when it comes to formulating a strategy.'

'Nick,' said the MD calmly, 'Take it from me, we all know what we mean.'

'Aha!' cried Nick triumphantly, 'You're playing the "We All Know What We Mean" game!'

'That's right,' said the MD cheerfully. 'And you are playing the "I'll Hold Up the Action By Being A Real Pain In The Arse" game. *Please* sit down, Nick.'

Advice to Nick

It sounds to me as if your MD was right; you *were* playing games!

Why, I wonder, do you find it necessary to confront people with such relish? Confronting people is dodgy enough, doing it with such obvious enjoyment is bound to aggravate. Accusing people of playing games when they are already feeling mystified and/or irritated is pretty well guaranteed to alienate.

It seems that you are overlooking your own assertion about effective communication – that the transmitter, not the receiver, has primary responsibility. When you confront people, causing widespread confusion and resentment, *you* are the transmitter. By your own reckoning, therefore, you, and you alone, must shoulder the blame for the negative reactions that ensue.

The answer is for you to overhaul your skills as a facilitator – especially the skills involved in intervening and giving helpful feedback. At present your style is likely to be perceived as aggressive; you pitch in with a judgement that implies you know best and that the other person is ignorant or just plain stupid. (If adding 'you idiot' fits nicely at the end of a sentence, you can be sure it was an aggressive statement.) This is bound to create unnecessary resistance.

Judgements of any kind are to be avoided if you want to maximise the probability of your interventions making a difference for the better (nothing will *guarantee* that you will be heeded). You'd be far better off sticking to neutral, as opposed to judgmental, descriptions of what is happening.

Non-judgmental feedback is a straightforward statement of what is, not what ought to be. For example, you said, '*You ought to agree what this word means. A shared understanding is absolutely essential before you move on.*' This is clearly judgmental with 'ought' and 'absolutely essential' looming large. A less aggressive way of making your intervention would have been to say something like, '*I notice that some of you are using this word in different ways. Before you move on, might it be worth spending a few minutes agreeing a working definition?*' The first sentence is an honest description of what you have observed and the second sentence suggests a way forward recognising that they have a choice.

So, next time, before you intervene, give yourself time to expunge all *shoulds*, *oughts* and *musts* from your vocabulary. Think of yourself as a mirror that merely offers a reflection without any judgement. Just stick to a simple two-sentence formula; your observation followed by your recommendation. The worst that can happen is that you will be ignored! Certainly, the risk of confrontation and outright rejection will have been massively reduced.

You could also make it a personal rule to stop accusing people of playing games. Think it if you must, but don't *say* it.

27

A manager who sampled 360 degree feedback and promptly went into denial

Ben was a middle manager in the purchasing department of a company that manufactured tyres for the motor industry. He worked in a large, draughty Victorian building that, despite refurbishment, still showed its age. The purchasing office was tucked away in one wing of the building along with other administrative functions. The bulk of the site, however, was given over to tyre manufacture – a dirty process. The manufacturing areas looked as if they belonged to another epoch.

There were two distinct categories of employee working on the site. About a quarter were salaried staff paid monthly and the rest were hourly-rated labourers paid weekly. The hourly-rated entered the building by a different entrance where they had to clock in. They also ate in a different canteen. The rationale for this segregation was that the hourly-rated workers were grubby and sweaty and salaried staff, many of them women, would not want to share the same facilities for fear of dirtying their clothes. It was also argued that the blue-collar workers preferred to take their breaks with their own kind, where they could relax, smoke and swear without feeling constrained or incurring displeasure.

In this predominantly macho environment, Ben cut an incongruous figure. A tall, dapper man, with spectacles dangling on a cord round his neck, he had a polite word for everybody. He was a well-read, well-travelled man with a love of opera and other things aesthetic. He was a leading light of the local choral society and a keen stamp collector. His job took him abroad three or four times a year on visits to rubber plantations in remote places (he was an expert on rubber production). Somehow Ben managed to disregard the pictures of naked and scantily clad girls that plastered walls and lockers throughout the manufacturing areas.

Ben had a small team of purchasing officers working for him, but he found the business of managing other people somewhat distasteful. He much preferred to leave them to their own devices and operate on the basis of 'no news is good news'. He called it managing by exception. In truth, he was much happier in his role as a specialist – an expert in rubber production with an industry-wide reputation.

Ben was therefore alarmed when he heard that the company was recasting the appraisal system and introducing 360-degree appraisals for all the managers. He went to a management briefing session run by an outside consultant – an American who worked for the company that was to supply the 360-degree package and provide the backup. Despite the consultant enthusing about the benefits of wholeheartedly embracing 360-degree feedback, Ben didn't like the sound of it at all. He considered it inappropriate and intrusive. How could his staff, or even his colleagues and bosses, assess him fairly given the specialist nature of his work?

Ben wrote a memo to his immediate boss, the purchasing director, arguing that specialists and professionals should be exempted from the scheme. It should be for 'proper' line managers. Predictably, the reply was that, in addition to being a specialist, Ben *was* a 'proper' manager and stood to learn from the feedback.

So, with a heavy heart, Ben filled in the detailed 'self' questionnaires indicating, from a list of 39 competencies, which he thought were critically important in the light of his current responsibilities, and assessing his skill levels against each competency. In addition to his manager, he elected to receive feedback from his five direct reports and two colleagues in neighbouring departments who knew him well.

After a couple of weeks, Ben's report arrived. It was 30 pages long with charts comparing the way he had rated himself with the way other people had rated him, followed by specific suggestions for development (in priority order) and a vast amount of supporting data. Ben was horrified to see that his manager had a completely different perception of which competencies were important. Ben, for example, had picked out competencies such as 'Functional Expertise', 'Recognising Global Implications' and 'Commitment to Quality' whereas his boss had earmarked items like 'Provide Direction', 'Motivate Others', and 'Coach and Develop'. Clearly this indicated some significant misunderstandings between him and his boss.

Furthermore, Ben was very hurt when he saw that, though his colleagues had rated his skills highly, his subordinates had marked him down in many areas, particularly the people-management aspects that his boss thought so important.

After the shock, denial set in as Ben became more and more convinced that he had suffered a terrible injustice. He decided to lodge an official complaint and demanded an early meeting with the purchasing director.

The purchasing director greeted him cordially and Ben let fly with his complaint – the gist of which was that the 360-degree system failed to take any account of his undoubted professional expertise. The director heard him out patiently with an 'I've-heard-all-this-before' smile on his face. When Ben had finished, the director opened the top left-hand drawer of his desk, drew out a single sheet of paper, and slid it over the desk to Ben.

'Tell me, Ben,' said the director, 'which of these apply to you?'

The sheet of paper was headed: *360-degree feedback – indicators of denial*. It went on to list the following:

- 'My job makes me act this way – I'm not really like this.'

- 'All my strengths are accurate but they've got my weaknesses wrong.'

- 'My job is so specialised that it is impossible for ordinary mortals to understand it.'

- 'I used to be this way but I've changed recently.'

- 'The wrong people obviously filled out the questionnaires.'

- 'My boss marked me down because he/she doesn't like me.'

- 'I wasn't like this in my last job.'

- 'I have global responsibilities and my respondents don't speak English very well.'

- 'It's just that I have a reputation to keep up; I'm actually much nicer than this.'

- 'I purposely picked people who don't like me.'

- 'People are jealous of my success.'

- 'This must be someone else's report.'

- 'The computer must have scored this wrong.'

It was Ben's turn to smile. And, to give him his due, he did!

Advice to Ben

You won't want to hear this, but your boss is right; you *are* a manager as well as a specialist.

The poor feedback from your staff is entirely understandable – they were, after all, rating you against managerial competencies. The 360 degree appraisal process has exposed you for what you are – not only a reluctant but also a neglectful manager.

You are not alone in retaining strong preferences for your professional work such that you neglect your managerial duties. Managing by exception is just a fancy way to mask what is effectively abdication. Every manager, in a previous existence, excelled at a specialism of some kind which had to be slowly relinquished as they transferred from being solely responsible for their own work to being responsible for the work of others. It sounds as if you have been allowed to side-step this transition.

The answer, I think, is to find ways to make you less neglectful and let your reluctance shrink as you gradually experience some positive reinforcement for your efforts. I'm gambling that once you've enjoyed some positive feedback, your willingness to manage will be strengthened. Putting it crudely; if at first you can't make it, fake it.

We need to find some actions, no more than three I suggest, that will give you some early successes. They also need to be things that you can do relatively easily. If they are too scary or demanding you'll quickly revert and we'll be back to square one. The 360-degree feedback you have received would be a good place to start – paying particular attention to the three areas your boss identified as important; providing direction, motivating staff, coaching and development.

Start by going through the development suggestions in the report you have received. Choose just one for each of the three competencies – all of them must be specific things you can realistically commit to doing at least, say, once a week. Examples might be:

- Meet with a member of your team to discuss their role and find out what extra help they'd like from you. Keep going at the rate of one team member a week until you have seen everyone then start all over again with progress reviews.

- Ask your staff for their ideas on ways to improve the efficiency of the purchasing office. And, of course, accept and implement as many ideas as you can.

- When you have an idea, consult the purchasing officers and use them as sounding boards.

- Ask your staff what skills they'd like to develop and get them to come up with ideas on how best to meet their needs.

- Review assignments by asking your staff for their 'wells and betters'. You only need two questions; what went well and what could have gone better.

- Get your team together for a learning review. Simply ask each person to come ready to share an example of an experience at work from which they have learned and, in the light of it, what they are planning to do better or differently.

Nothing here is rocket science – that's the whole point, to have simple, practical things you can do that will make an impact.

When you have chosen your three actions, discuss them with your manager. This has three purposes. Firstly, to 'advertise' your determination to improve your management practices. Secondly, to enlist his support and see if he can build on your ideas. Thirdly, to bolster your resolve to implement the actions.

Once you start doing these things on a weekly basis you'll find it isn't half as bad as you thought and you might even start to enjoy being a manager.

28

A manager who thought brainstorming was the answer to just about everything

Miles was a section manager in a large design agency. He was in his thirties, with an unkempt beard and given to wearing corduroy trousers. He had a degree in graphics and design and was a gifted cartoonist. The agency created advertising campaigns, advised on corporate logos and designed catalogues and brochures for a number of blue-chip companies. The ethos of the place was right-brained, informal and emphatically 'can do'.

Miles was a great fan of intuitive processes and lateral thinking. He was fascinated by the way ideas would pop into his head when he was least expecting them. Blinding flashes of inspiration would visit him in the shower or when cruising along a motorway and, sometimes, in the middle of the night. Besides listening to these unexpected voices, he also set great store by freewheeling sessions where he would encourage people to think 'off the top of the head'. This was the equivalent of playing a word-association game. Miles would urge the participants to think wild and aim at quantity, not quality. Sometimes, when the stream of ideas dried up, he'd indulge in some random stimulation to 'get the creative juices flowing again'. This involved taking hold of a dictionary and asking someone to call out two numbers. The first was the number of the page Miles would turn to and the second was the word on that page. Whatever word this process threw up – the more obscure the better – it would be used to unleash another torrent of thoughts.

Miles was very fond of techniques like this to free up his own and others' thinking. Sometimes he'd produce a photograph from a newspaper or magazine and invite people to suggest an original caption. Brainstorming was another technique that he'd inflict on his team at the drop of a hat. He'd suddenly say, 'Let's brainstorm this', and stand eagerly at the whiteboard, marker poised, ready to record *verbatim* whatever ideas emerged.

Some members of the team responded well to these brainstorming sessions. They seemed happy to suspend judgement and spontaneously call out their ideas. Others, however, would remain virtually silent and sit, looking embarrassed, waiting for normal business to resume. The more Miles urged them to join in and 'think outside the box', the more tight-lipped they became. Sometimes, in desperation, Miles would halt the brainstorm, seize any nearby object – a paperclip, for example, or a glass, or a pair of scissors – and say, looking pointedly at the quieter folk, 'In how many ways could we use this?' Unfortunately, far from re-balancing contribution rates, this would be a signal for the more verbose members of the team to fire off a rapid salvo of bizarre ideas.

One day Miles imposed yet another instant brainstorming session onto his team but, after only five minutes or so, they were interrupted by a call from Miles' boss who wanted to see him urgently. As Miles dashed off, he suggested that they reconvene the next day and continue where they had left off.

Sure enough, the next day Miles called together the team to conclude the brainstorming session they had started. Miles was astonished to notice that the members of the team who were normally tongue-tied now produced a deluge of ideas. Indeed, the person who usually said nothing at all rattled off a dozen ideas that stimulated some promising cross-fertilisation. Miles was delighted but puzzled.

After the meeting, Miles made a point of commenting on the success of the brainstorm to two of the team members who were normally quiet. They agreed that it had gone well and said they'd enjoyed it more than usual.

'But why?' asked Miles, 'Why was it different?'

'It was because we had time to marshal our thoughts and generate some ideas in our own time', explained Sam, who was invariably struck dumb by brainstorms. 'You see, brainstorming suits spontaneous people. But if you are the sort of person who likes time to reflect without undue pressure, then brainstorming is over before you're ready to begin.'

Miles was staggered by this revelation. It had never previously occurred to him that the brainstorming technique was discriminatory.

Advice to Miles

You've rediscovered that one size does not fit all. It is always much easier to proceed on the assumption that everyone is the same. The fact that people differ is endlessly fascinating but administratively *very* inconvenient!

There are many practices, happening on a daily basis in most organisations, that have built-in biases that favour some and disadvantage others. Besides brainstorming (of which more in a moment), examples are the tendency to:

- standardise rules, regulations and procedures;

- insist on one business language;

- select articulate people who perform well in interviews;

- promote people who are charismatic and extroverted;

- expect people to speak up and compete for airtime in meetings and discussions;

- use one consistent management style regardless of the circumstances;

- assume that fairness is treating everyone the same;

- offer people incentives irrespective of their needs.

All these tendencies, and many others like them, unintentionally discriminate against some people and prevent them from participating as effectively as they might. People differ in all sorts of ways – some of them immediately obvious such as height, weight, gender, dress and skin colour, and others less obvious such as their background, beliefs and attitudes, knowledge and interests, skills and abilities, behaviour and personality. The goal is to turn differences such as these to advantage by valuing diversity, i.e. creating the conditions where difference does not stop people from participating.

Valuing diversity rests on the assumption that *everyone*, without exception, has potentially useful ideas to contribute and that it is up to you actively to solicit those ideas. The belief is that the quality of decisions increases in direct proportion to the number of different ideas generated. The greater the diversity, the better the eventual decision.

Brainstorming is another example of an approach that is unwittingly discriminatory. The technique suits people who are relatively happy to go at risk and generate ideas in quick, spontaneous bursts. People who prefer to mull things over and allow their ideas to emerge in their own time, without pressure, are seriously handicapped under the relatively manic conditions imposed by brainstorming. Insisting they think wild, cross-fertilise and go for quantity, not quality, is, for them, counterproductive. The more you urge reflective types on, the more inhibited they are likely to become.

The solution, as you have already discovered, is simple; give the members of your team due notice of an idea-generating session and the topic/problem to be addressed. This gives people with different temperaments a choice; they can prepare ideas in advance or not depending on their preferred way of working.

It is worth checking out other things you do that might militate against people participating as fully as they might. Since you already have diversity in your team, you might as well work out how to use it to add value.

29

A manager who couldn't resist tinkering with written reports

David was a civil servant who worked at a government establishment in the open countryside. He was a dapper little man with a neat moustache and round 'Schubert' spectacles that used to look old fashioned but are now in great demand.

David had two notable characteristics. Firstly, he was a keen bird watcher and always had a pair of binoculars with him. The grounds of the government installation where David worked were extensive (the site of a World War II airfield) and featured many mature trees. David would spend his lunchtimes wandering through the grounds looking at birds and entering details of his various sightings in a pocket notebook. In his office was a much more powerful pair of binoculars mounted on a tripod. He'd always have half an eye on the window and, disconcertingly, he'd suddenly break off a conversation and rush to the binoculars and train them on some bird that had just come into view.

Secondly, David was fastidious when it came to words and grammar. His tendency towards over-precision was, quite possibly, involuntary since his grandfather had been part of a celebrated team that had worked on a revision of *The Oxford English Dictionary*. David was addicted to (in this order) his grandfather's dictionary, *Roget's Thesaurus*, *The Oxford Dictionary of Quotations* and the crossword in *The Times*. If he completed the crossword, he would be in a good mood; if he didn't he was irritable.

David had some pet hates – not individuals but expressions. For example, if someone said, 'You know', David would say pointedly, 'No, I do *not*.' If someone said, 'Have a nice day' David would puff himself up and say, 'Thank you, but I have other plans.' If someone said, 'OK?' rhetorically at the end of a sentence, David would make a point of saying, 'No, it is not' (he couldn't bring himself to say, 'No, it isn't'). Since the OK was an automatic reflex on the part of the speaker, David's calculated response, after three or four repetitions, invariably brought the conversation to a halt.

David's subordinates were frequently required to submit detailed written reports giving the results of investigations. David insisted on personally signing off each report before it left the department. This gave David the opportunity (an opportunity he relished!) to check the grammar and punctuation. Of course, he always found it necessary to make corrections. Sometimes it was inserting a comma here and there, sometimes breaking up long sentences into smaller ones and sometimes it meant rewriting complete sections. David made these alterations in red and tossed the offending report back to the author for correction.

As you can imagine, David's subordinates resented having their reports rejected in this way – especially when it was necessary to rewrite long passages and resubmit them to David. Sometimes a report would become trapped in an endless loop as David edited it again and again seeking perfection.

One of David's subordinates decided to conduct some damage limitation experiments. He drew up a list of some of David's pet hates – missed apostrophes, split infinitives, direct questions with no question mark, commas rather than semicolons, and excessive use of brackets, words like data, criteria and phenomena treated as singular – and so on. He found that if he deliberately inserted three or four of these errors in a report, it came back with far fewer corrections than before.

Having made the discovery that David must have *something* to change, and that his pet hates were guaranteed to attract his attention, everyone started to use the 'deliberate mistakes' ploy. David, the purist, was happy (whether he ever realised what was happening is uncertain). And so were his subordinates, who enjoyed a dramatic decrease in irksome rewrites.

Advice to David

You are clearly a stickler for detail who finds it difficult, if not impossible, to trust people to write reports that match your high standards. It is interesting to speculate about your motives. I can think of three possibilities.

1. You are keen to ensure that your customers receive well-written, accurate reports.

2. You are keen to show your staff the error of their ways and thus train them up to be more careful with their written work.

3. You get a real buzz out of making corrections with your red pen and demonstrating your superiority.

These are not mutually exclusive – all three could apply.

However, it may not have occurred to you that your insistence on checking each report before it is issued, is exactly the wrong thing to do if you want to achieve 2 in the above list. Far from training your staff to be more careful, you are actually sheltering them from the harsh realities of taking responsibility for the accuracy of their own work. All you are doing is training them to rely on you. Why would they bother to do any quality assurance when they know you'll be fastidious in spotting and correcting all their mistakes? You may think you are being a hard task-master, but in fact you are unwittingly providing them with a soft option; to produce sloppy work in the sure knowledge that you will sort it out!

You can solve this problem very easily. Simply issue a policy directive that says that in future you want your staff to take responsibility for the quality of their written reports and that you will only check them *after they have gone to the customer*. This will give them an incentive to produce accurate work and satisfy your need to do some hands-on checking. It will also make it more likely that, when you consider a report to have fallen below standard, instead of behaving like a disgruntled schoolmaster, you will coach the author and help them to see how to improve.

I'm not suggesting that you lower your standards, only that you maintain them by modifying your approach. The secret of success is to review the reports *after* they have gone, not *before* they go. This may strike you as risky, but it is the only way to break the cycle and wean your staff off their dependence on you.

If you implement this change of approach you will find the reports your staff produce are increasingly satisfactory. You will then have the confidence to throttle back and content yourself with only checking a sample – or confine yourself to reviewing only the most complex or the most important reports. This will ease your workload.

Eventually you may even reach a stage where it is safe to leave each author to do their own quality assurance. Exactly what managers are for!

30

A story about two managers vying for promotion

Paul and Harry worked in a large science laboratory. The laboratory had contracts with governments and manufacturing companies throughout the world. They specialised in analytical technology in areas such as food, pharmaceuticals, environmental pollution, health and safety and forensics. The laboratory employed some 600 scientists, many of them graduates in their first jobs.

Paul's and Harry's backgrounds were remarkably similar. They were both chemists with PhDs. They were both recruited on the same university 'milk round' and even shared the same starting date at the laboratory. They were both in their late 30s, married, with mortgages and young families. They headed parallel departments specialising in different business sectors and were both well thought of and earmarked for promotion.

There were, however, a number of ways in which they differed. Their personalities, for example. Paul was analytical and calm whereas Harry, despite his training as a scientist, was intuitive and flamboyant. These tendencies naturally affected the way they approached their work. Paul, when faced with a problem, would reflect and 'sleep on it'. Harry would rush in, impatient to find a quick solution. Paul was quiet and thoughtful at management meetings. When he spoke, people listened because they knew he would offer a considered opinion. Harry, on the other hand, was cheerfully spontaneous, with much to say, happy to speculate and think out loud. It was Harry who would volunteer to speak at conferences or to rush round the country visiting universities on a recruitment drive.

Despite their different temperaments, the men were friendly and co-operative to one another. They each respected the other's skills. It was a splendid example of the attraction of opposites. They often conferred together about how best to deal with awkward situations in their respective teams. Paul appreciated the way Harry would urge him to take decisive action earlier than he otherwise would. And there were numerous occasions when Harry benefited from Paul's wise counsel not to act before he had gathered some more facts.

Paul's approach was heavily influenced by the teachings of the late W Edwards Deming, the quality guru. Paul totally subscribed to Deming's ideas about the importance of processes and the need to understand the causes of underlying variances. He was a keen advocate of statistical process control, and flow diagrams, Pareto analyses and control charts were much in evidence in his laboratory.

Naturally Paul did his best to persuade Harry to adopt the same disciplines in his laboratory, but Harry was resistant. He argued that problems provided the challenges that made life interesting; preventing problems was merely boring. Harry would gently tease Paul by asking him if his charts showed him how many problems he was preventing. He was adamant that you never acquired merit by preventing problems – only by fixing them.

'That's what managers are for, to solve problems' Harry would say. 'If there weren't any problems you'd be redundant.'

Paul's faith in prevention being better than cure was, if anything,

155

strengthened by Harry's taunts. He was confident that it was worthwhile and he continued to pore over histograms and scatter diagrams in a bid to detect and reduce defects in his laboratory's working processes. So convinced was he that the Deming approach made sense that he produced a paper for the board based on Deming's Fourteen Points for Management. The paper was presented at a meeting but the directors struggled with much of the philosophy. They couldn't envisage a workplace that eliminated inspection and replaced it with a culture that made employees responsible for the quality of their work. A particular sticking point was the idea that fear must be driven out of the workplace. This suggestion provoked an outbreak of denial as director after director insisted that fear was not an issue in the organisation.

After a few weeks, it was announced that Paul's and Harry's immediate boss was going to take a year's sabbatical. This was quite unexpected and not normal practice. It transpired that their boss wanted time to write a book and, after many years of service, had negotiated a special arrangement with the board. Paul and Harry were the obvious contenders to take over in his absence. It was clearly a splendid opportunity to enjoy higher visibility with senior management and establish their credentials for a permanent position.

Both Paul and Harry were invited to give a presentation to the board showing why the job should be theirs. The gist of Paul's case was that he had saved the company money and enhanced quality by focusing on prevention and continuous improvement. Harry's case was that he was a proven problem-solver and effective decision-maker.

It was no contest. Harry got the job and, to his credit, resisted the temptation to say 'I told you so'.

Advice to Paul

We need to make sure that next time you make a better impression.

Prevention is undoubtedly better than cure and in a perfect world this would be recognised and beyond dispute. Indeed, the very existence of a problem would be regarded as an indictment – a failure to have taken the steps necessary to prevent it.

However, as you know only too well, the world is not perfect and there is a tendency for problems to grab the headlines and for the people who succeed in fixing them to be regarded as heroes. The difficulty, as your colleague Harry has pointed out, is that problems tend to be dramatic and highly visible whereas preventing problems is for the most part routine and largely invisible. The absence of something doesn't make as much impact as the presence of something. It is much more difficult to boast about something that didn't happen than something that did! Also, absurd as it may sound, many people are attracted to problems. They find them exciting, challenging and intriguing. They love the flurry of activity, the thrill of crisis management and the accolades that follow when a problem has been solved. These people may be so addicted to problems that they actually *create them* as an antidote to a boring world where everything runs smoothly.

Despite the 'popularity' of problems, making an intellectual case for their prevention is relatively easy. Anyone in their right minds can see that problems are costly of time, effort and money and that it would be preferable to prevent them. But depriving people of their emotional attachment to problems, and the highs they get from tackling them, is quite another matter. Problems win every time.

So, assuming you don't want to do a complete U turn and abandon the preventative processes you have carefully put in place, what can you do? The answer, I think, is to stop being such a purist. Presumably, problems sometimes occur, both in your laboratory and in the organisation as a whole. You'll have to use them to cultivate a reputation as a problem solver, not just a problem preventer. I'm *not* suggesting you engineer problems so that you can demonstrate your prowess at fixing them; just that you make more of the problems that crop up in the normal course of events.

When there is a problem in your laboratory, i.e. a difference between what you want and what you've got, think of it as an opportunity to enhance your reputation. Discuss the problem and, even more importantly, *your proposed solution* with your boss. Make presentations at management meetings where you show how you analysed and solved the problem. Expose problems that are facing the organisation as a whole – not just the parochial ones in your laboratory – and volunteer to lead a task force to investigate the causes of the problem and come up with some recommended actions.

In other words, look to your own PR and use problems as opportunities to raise your profile and enhance your reputation.

31

A manager who found it convenient to disappear for long periods

Mike was head of IT in a local authority. He was based in the Civic Offices – a large modern office block in the city centre. The authority had already outgrown this building by the time it was officially opened, and the overspill were housed in a hotchpotch of older buildings scattered around the city.

Mike was an affable fellow who very much enjoyed moving about. If a problem arose, his inclination was to jump in his car and go and see for himself. He hated days when he was cooped up in his office, talking on the phone and attending to emails. He also loathed formal meetings with an agenda and minutes and all the other paraphernalia. He maintained that far more could be accomplished by an informal chat and that many problems could be nipped in the bud if you went to deal with them in person before they had a chance to worsen.

Mike's secretary was a long-suffering woman called Alice. Alice led a stressful existence because, although the IT function was supported by a helpline, she used to receive irate calls from frustrated users when they encountered problems of various kinds. Mike's frequent, unscheduled disappearing acts were another cause of Alice's suffering. Despite her remonstrations, he rarely troubled to tell her where he was going or for how long he might be away. Her office was immediately next to his, but he had a door that led directly onto the corridor. When she realised that nagging wasn't working, she gave him a pager – but he used to forget to take it or, if he took it, he turned it off. Mike treated his mobile phone with the same disdain. If he had it with him, and if it rang or vibrated, he'd simply turn it off and carry on with whatever he was doing.

Alice was annoyed about his absences because they used to reflect on her. She resented being made to look inefficient through no fault of her own. During one of Mike's escapes, people would demand to know where he was and when he would be back. Sometimes she would hazard a guess only to find that she had grossly underestimated the length of his absence. Sometimes she would confess that she had lost him and had no idea when he might return. Sometimes she would promise to locate him and telephone likely places until she tracked him down. But the process was time-consuming and made her appear disorganised. People would even tease her with taunts of 'Lost him again then?'

One day, after a particularly trying spate of absences, Alice talked the situation over with a colleague – another senior secretary she often joined for lunch. They reviewed her options. Force Mike to make his escapes via her office by locking his outer door onto the corridor. Padlock him to his desk. Immobilise his car. Move into his office. Train a security camera on his door to monitor his movements. Fit a siren to the door so that whenever it opened it made a wailing noise.

Though some of the options were tempting, they seemed inappropriate or far-fetched. The two women fell to thinking about more feasible ways to solve the problem. As they struggled to think of ideas, Alice's colleague began to wonder if they could adopt a 'carrot and stick' approach. Was there some way of making Mike's life inconvenient when he disappeared without telling Alice where he was going? And, by contrast, was there a way to make his life more convenient when he did tell her?

Suddenly, Alice had an inspiration! She realised that whenever Mike vanished, she used to prepare a neat list of all his messages, with the names and numbers of the people he needed to call back, and brief him on his return. She also realised that if something urgent cropped up, she'd ring around doing her utmost to track him down. In other words, Alice, by being conscientious, was *rewarding* him when he returned from an unscheduled absence.

Together the two secretaries hatched a plan. If Mike told Alice where he was going, she would continue to provide the usual service. If he disappeared without telling her, she would busy herself with other tasks and not bother to take messages or compile a list. Nor would she try to track him down with any urgent messages. In this way, she'd reward Mike when he had the courtesy to inform her of his whereabouts and punish him when he didn't.

Alice explained her plan to Mike and he chuckled, appreciating the ingenuity of the scheme. For a while he even remembered to put his head round Alice's door and tell her where he was off to and how long he might be. But the day came when he rushed away to tackle some problem and forgot to inform Alice. So, fighting back her impulse to be super-efficient in his absence, she implemented the plan.

She only had to do it once and Mike, at long last, learnt his lesson.

Advice to Mike

Alice is impressive and clearly capable of taking on much more responsibility. You are very fortunate to have such a resourceful assistant and I suspect that her talents are under-utilised. I'm confident that, if she had the authority, she could do much more to deputise for you when you are away from your desk. How about reviewing Alice's current job with a view to promoting her and/or getting her job upgraded?

Have a chat with Alice to establish whether she would like to take on more and, if so, what. In preparation, ask Alice to draw up a comprehensive list of what she currently does and another of what she would like to do if she had the time. Sit down with Alice and compare the two lists. Are there tasks she does at present that could be streamlined or ditched? Are there additional tasks that you both agree she could do? Do they match the things she says she would like to do?

Sort things into four categories:

• Things Alice could start doing.

• Things Alice could stop doing.

• Things Alice could do more of.

• Things Alice could do less of.

Then ask Alice to write her own job description and submit it for re-grading. I hope you agree that she must be suitably reimbursed for any extra responsibilities she takes on. There is no question of exploiting her efficiency and good nature.

32

A manager who perfected resistance by inertia

Derek was a middle manager in a software house with an international presence.

He was an easy-going fellow who liked to take the line of least resistance. His relaxed style was partly explained by his dread of anything that smacked of confrontation. He was a past master at smoothing ruffled feathers and (to offer a choice of metaphors!) pouring oil on troubled waters. If he couldn't prevent upsets with diplomacy and charm, he simply reverted to plan B, which was to avoid the problem, or the person, until the difficulty resolved itself.

In fact, Derek was a great believer in taking no action and waiting to see what would happen. He found that, more often than not, crises simply fizzled out or events were overtaken by something fortuitous. Each time this occurred, it reinforced his preference for biding his time and doing nothing.

Over the years, Derek's inertia had successfully seen off many initiatives. He had dragged his feet when the company went through a phase of setting up quality circles (the champion of this venture suddenly left the company to join the firm of management consultants who were masterminding the initiative). He had also survived crazes for management by objectives, process re-engineering, statistical process control, 360-degree feedback, what-if scenario planning and numerous cost-cutting exercises. If each one had been a notch on Derek's belt, they would have stretched half-way around his generous waist.

Derek's resistance by stealth always followed a set pattern. When the initiative was first mooted, he would respond in such a way that people assumed he was in agreement. He'd sit back, listening to different points of view, and do his best to remain on the fence. Most times this simply meant not expressing any reservations rather than having to display any pretence of support or enthusiasm. It was extraordinary how a few judicious nods of the head, and a carefully placed smile here and there, would allow him to escape close scrutiny.

The next phase, after a period of acquiescence, usually meant postponing whatever actions he was supposed to be taking. He found that by doing nothing he could spin things out – certainly for weeks, sometimes for months – before questions were asked. Quite often, questions were never asked because priorities had changed and something else was now in vogue. If Derek *was* called to account, he would concoct a plausible sounding excuse and win more time by implementing a few of the preliminary steps. He would take some token actions that were relatively inconsequential and easily reversed. This took the pressure off and bought him time. The aim was to stretch the process out until all momentum was lost and/or the instigators of the initiative gave up or disappeared.

The company was American-owned and one day yet another important initiative was announced by the HQ in Chicago; it was decreed that diversity was an increasing issue now that the company operated in so many different countries, and a diversity awareness programme was to be launched. The new head of diversity explained, on the all-singing-all-dancing diversity website, that the one-day programme (spelt program) would be rolled out world-wide and that attendance by management and staff in every country would be compulsory. There were to be no exceptions.

The board were persuaded to demonstrate their commitment to diversity by attending the programme themselves. They all emerged with imposing comments about the need to stay competitive by valuing diversity and that, aside from the commercial benefits, it was 'the right thing to do'. The CEO even made a video underlining the importance of diversity awareness and giving examples of disasters that had occurred in different markets because diversity issues had been overlooked. None of the examples were home grown – they had all been drawn from the experiences of other companies and competitors!

Naturally, Derek identified this as another initiative that would have to be stifled by inertia. However, he saw no alternative but to attend the launch programme in the UK. It was delivered by two American consultants who made no concessions to local circumstances, and were completely dismissive of the sound work that had been done over a number of years, in conjunction with the staff unions, on equal opportunities. Derek lay low, as usual, as his colleagues on the programme started to raise objections and show their displeasure at the arrogant stand being taken by the two consultants. But Derek was surprised to find himself getting genuinely annoyed. He became crosser and crosser as he dwelt on the irony and the arrogance of a programme extolling the virtues of diversity that made no allowances for local conditions.

Eventually, Derek could stand it no longer. To the astonishment of his colleagues, he stood up and told the consultants that the diversity programme was an insult and that it was doomed to failure unless the

165

messages were tailored to take account of the culture of different countries – starting with the UK. 'One size does not fit all,' he roared. 'Surely, this is the whole point of valuing diversity?'

The programme broke up in disarray. The message went back to the States and the programme was suspended 'pending further consideration'.

When the MD of the UK company next saw Derek at a company function, he went out of his way to thank him for putting his head above the parapet. No one seemed to have noticed that this was completely out of character.

Advice to Derek

Splendid – you have spoken up and succeeded in stopping something foolish in its tracks. And, deservedly, you have received congratulations for making a stand.

Is this experience enough to wean you off your usual tactic of hiding your reservations and lying low? Just think of the time and energy you'd save if you took decisive action and nipped things in the bud. Letting poor initiatives limp on, starved of the oxygen of support, is a waste of everyone's resources.

When you first hear about a new idea or initiative, limit your response to one of the following:

- If you think it has merit, say so, giving specific examples of what you like about it.

- If you think it is daft, say so, and give a reason – singular. It is important to confine yourself to one reservation at a time. If you blurt out lots of reasons, people tend to pick on the weakest one and ignore the others.

- If you aren't sure, say so and give an indication of when you will be ready to offer an opinion. Simply say something like, 'Hmm … I'd like time to think about that. I'll let you know by (date/time).'

Notice that implying consent by staying silent is not an option! Confining yourself to just three possibilities – yes, no, not sure – will help to get you off the fence and, hopefully, win you more accolades. It is astonishing how, if you have the courage to speak up, other people will come out in support. They just need someone to start the ball rolling.

33

A manager who was reluctant to go home

Adam was the training manager of a travel company. He had an extensive knowledge of the travel industry and could rattle off numerous statistics going back over many years. As you might guess, Adam was an intense character. His attempts at light-hearted banter were simply embarrassing. His sense of humour, if indeed one existed, was so obscure that other people failed to see it.

With his impressive store of knowledge, Adam was a 'must' on every induction programme for new staff. Though not a natural performer, he always rose to the occasion. He used numerous PowerPoints showing graphs and trends in business contrasted with leisure travel, etc. He also used a quiz he had compiled with a series of questions, each of which had a counter-intuitive answer. No one could ever survive it and Adam would swell with pride as he demonstrated his superior expertise.

Unfortunately Adam was so dedicated to his job that he was loath to go home. A less charitable theory was that he hated his wife and/or didn't want to arrive home before the kids were safely tucked up in bed! Anyway, whatever the explanation, Adam used to linger on after the official finishing time of 5.30 pm.

If he had been content to confine his lingering to his own office, poring over statistics, all would have been well. The trouble was, Adam had developed a habit of wandering down the corridor about ten minutes before finishing time and dropping into someone else's office for a chat. And could he chat! Words flowed out of him in a steady, unbroken stream, as unstoppable as water running downhill. There was no escape. If he happened to arrive in your office, short of saying your grandmother was on her deathbed and that her dying wish was to see you for the last time, you were stuck. (People soon ran out of grandmothers!)

Gradually people – with kids they liked to read stories to at bedtime and partners they wanted to make love to – came to deeply resent the inconvenience of Adam's delaying tactics. So a plot was hatched. Everyone who had an office within Adam's range joined in drawing up a roster. The person whose name was at the top of the roster had to be a sacrificial offering and, no later than 5.10 pm, devise some pretext for going to see Adam in his office. There the unfortunate person would have to engage Adam in conversation so that everyone else could leave for home promptly at 5.30.

The plan to distract Adam was a triumph and, so far as anyone knows, he never caught on.

Advice to Adam

I will not pry into your reasons for lingering in the office and postponing going home. They are your business. However, inconveniencing members of your staff is an unacceptable practice that will have to stop.

Perhaps you don't realise the resentment it causes when you saunter into someone's office close to the official finishing time? If so, you must be completely insensitive to the desperate signals being transmitted by your hapless victims; the crest fallen looks, the surreptitious glances at the clock, the way they stand in a bid to minimise the length of your stay, the monosyllabic answers, the one-sidedness of the conversation. All these behaviours, and others like them, are easy to observe.

I strongly recommend that you brush up on your empathetic skills. Start by putting yourself in other people's shoes and seeing things from their point of view. Imagine, for example:

1. you have done a hard days work;

2. you have young children who love being read to at bedtime;

3. the journey home takes at least 45 minutes;

4. in the normal course of events, barring emergencies, you finish work at 5.30 and it is now 5.15 or so;

5. your boss wanders into your office, sits down and starts chatting about inconsequential things that could easily wait until the morning.

How would you feel? Somewhat pissed off surely?

Practising empathy will help you to be a far more effective manager. You will be able to anticipate how people are likely to feel about all sorts of things and work out what you could do to minimise negative feelings that hinder people's performance. I say 'likely to feel' because different people react differently (even to the same event) and, of course, people are free to chose how they feel. But at least you can do a better job at appreciating how they are *likely* to feel. All you have to do is get into the habit of looking at things from different viewpoints. It will stop you being such an egocentric sod!

All this assumes that you are not being deliberately vindictive by holding your staff back when it is time to go home. If this is the explanation, then this is a form of bullying and you should not be surprised if turnover amongst your staff is high. They may find it easier to vote with their feet and be shot of you altogether than to walk out on you at 5.30 each evening and leave you talking to yourself.

34

An insecure manager clinging on for survival

Reg was an account manager in an advertising agency. He headed a team of creative young people who specialised in producing promotional materials for a variety of different clients. Reg was a failed architect who was good at drawing cartoons and had drifted into advertising simply because he had some useful contacts in that world via his brother-in-law.

Reg was in his early fifties and knew he had peaked. He felt increasingly vulnerable. He had no qualifications to speak of and was painfully aware that his team were all a) much younger than him b) graduates and c) more gifted than he was. He did his best to conceal his misgivings but each day he felt he was teetering on the very edge of his competence and the merest puff of wind could blow him over at any moment. He even had dreams about falling off Beachy Head with the Samaritans looking over the edge calling out belatedly, 'Think again!' Horrible feelings to harbour; energy-sapping to conceal.

Reg had developed a number of strategies for survival. One was to be extraordinarily positive with his team. When in their presence he took pains to appear casually confident. He was full of cheerful, macho banter and would gently ridicule their ideas as if they were naïve kids and he knew better. Another tactic was to take personal credit for his team's work. He often, for example, made appointments to meet clients but kept the time and place secret from those members of his team who, in normal circumstances, would have attended. And whenever the work of his team was subjected to any sort of internal review, he would glibly pass off other people's ideas as his own and leave the impression that the members of his team had merely done the groundwork.

Of course, his team members weren't stupid. They understood what was going on and deeply resented Reg's exploitation. However, they were at a loss to know what to do about it apart from remonstrating with Reg and making it clear they wanted credit where credit was due. He fobbed them off with assurances, but their protests only made him cleverer at keeping up the deception; essential for a man who knew he was hanging on by his finger-tips.

Then Reg fell ill. He experienced chest pains in the shower one morning and his wife, an ex-nurse, gave him aspirin and rushed him into hospital. The stress of keeping up pretences had taken its toll. Reg was kept in hospital for two weeks where he underwent various tests – blood pressure, cholesterol levels, scans, treadmills – the works. He was put on medication and allowed home. Doctors diagnosed high stress levels and told him to take things easy.

During Reg's enforced absence, his team members realised they had a golden opportunity to demonstrate their capabilities. They immediately fixed review meetings with their clients and deputised for Reg at meetings with senior management in the agency. They were careful not to criticise Reg, indeed they never mentioned him unless it was in answer to a direct question, but took every chance that came their way to claim ownership for their work.

When Reg returned after his sick leave he was mightily relieved to see that he still had a desk. On the second day back his boss sent for him.

Reg walked down the corridors of power convinced he was about to be sacked and arrived at his boss's office in a state of considerable agitation (not at all what the doctor ordered!).

'Reg!' said his boss, shaking him warmly by the hand. 'Very good to have you back. I just wanted to congratulate you on having such a splendid team. While you were away they rose to the occasion admirably. All credit to you for developing such a talented team.'

Reg reflected on this undeserved praise and, from that day forth, stopped hiding his team's talents and, instead, learned to bask in the reflected glory. *Much* better for his blood pressure.

Advice to Reg

It sounds as though you have learnt your lesson and finally realised that managing a team is all about providing nurture and support so that their capabilities are developed.

Feeling vulnerable is a widespread problem for many managers who have been promoted to their level of incompetence. This is known as The Peter Principle. You'll know from your own experience, that you were on top of things when, years ago, you were drawing cartoons but, now you have a bright, capable team to lead, you are out of your depth. Of course, it isn't the done thing to admit this so, inevitably, you pretend all is well and conceal your misgivings.

The extent to which a manager, in order to be competent, needs to be able to do well everything he or she requires of their staff is an interesting debating point. Increasingly, in an age of specialists and leading edge technologies, the answer tends to be that a manager needs to be competent at managing – not necessarily at operating. This means that a manager is, to a large extent, dependent on others – and for many this feeling of dependency is unsettling.

Managers who don't feel confident, worry that people might easily mislead them by blinding them with science. They also have a fear of looking foolish or inadequate in the eyes of their subordinates. By contrast, confident managers accept that they can't know it all and set about creating an environment at work where people will flourish and where their talents are allowed to make a difference.

So, hopefully, the penny has finally dropped and you are at peace with your primary role – to develop your people and take vicarious pleasure in their successes.

35

A manager with unquenchable enthusiasm

Chris was a manager in an oil refinery. It was the usual jumble of endless pipes, vast containers and flares and, like all managers in refineries, Chris had a large aerial photograph of the plant, in glorious colour, on his office wall. From the air, the refinery looked orderly and systematic – a place that must have been contrived with the aid of a set-square and spirit level.

Chris had a striking distinguishing feature – a generous shock of ginger hair (well, orange really) above a pale, heavily freckled face. His nickname was Tonic. This may seem puzzling but it can be explained. In Chris' school days his nickname was, unsurprisingly, Ginger. At university, gradually, in the lazy way people have with nicknames, it became shortened to Gin. And Gin reminded people of gin and tonic …

As it happens, Tonic was an appropriate label for Chris for another, quite unrelated, reason. You see, Chris was very much a morning person and was lively from the moment his head left the pillow. He would leap up, ready to seize the day, at 6 am. Swiftly pulling on some old clothes, he would rouse a reluctant dog and set off on a brisk walk. Everyone he met (mercifully not many that early in the morning) he greeted with unrestrained enthusiasm. Back from a three-mile walk, he would make a cup of tea for his wife (not a morning person, so still in bed) and then have a lukewarm shower and a vigorous rub down with a rough towel. Chris had acquired a taste for cool showers at his boarding school where cold, not merely cool, showers were the norm. (Another longstanding tradition at his school had been a rule that trouser pockets were sewn up. No wonder Chris exhibited some strange behaviour.)

The international oil-company Chris worked for frequently dispatched managers to the Lake District to participate in an Outward Bound training course. Leadership was the theme and the aim of the course was to increase participants' self-belief by setting them various physical challenges. There were orienteering exercises, long hikes on the fells, some rock climbing and some canoeing in fast-flowing water. The course culminated in an activity involving participants being dumped in the middle of nowhere, with a tent and meagre rations, and left to fend for themselves for three days.

This was exactly the sort of experience Chris relished and he was delighted when his turn came to undertake the training. Conditions at the Outward Bound centre were Spartan (no problem for Chris, just for everyone else!) and participants slept in dormitories with bunk beds. It was traditional to toss a coin to decide who would take the bottom bunk. As it happens, Chris lost the toss and was consigned to a top bunk. Ignorant of Chris' hyperactive tendencies, no one realised what a fearful mistake this would turn out to be – particularly for the person in the bottom bunk.

Despite the physical exertions of the first day of the course (they had walked miles over the fells as part of a mountain rescue exercise), Chris woke as early as usual and swung his legs over the edge of the bunk. This caused the bunk beds to wobble and the person in the bottom bunk woke with a start. He was faced with an extraordinary sight: Chris' cheerful face grinning down at him between two thin, pale legs covered in bright ginger hairs.

'New day, new opportunities!' shouted Chris with his customary enthusiasm, and he launched himself off the bunk and landed on the floor.

This extravagant behaviour repeated itself every morning, causing widespread distress to everyone in Chris' dormitory. Never had a group of managers been keener to embark on the three-day solitary exercise.

A few weeks after the course, each person in the dorm received a small parcel marked 'personal'. Inside was a hand-made mug bearing the slogan 'New day, new opportunities!' in large letters. It turned out that hyperactive Chris was an amateur potter. He just wanted to make sure that his colleagues took the message seriously.

Advice to Chris

I'm sure being an enthusiast is a characteristic you are proud to exhibit, but surely you must have noticed that some people find it difficult to stomach such unrestrained enthusiasm – especially first thing in the morning?

You probably *have* detected some reticence, but decided to ignore it and appoint yourself as cheerleader. In common with most 'morning people', you probably get a kick out of jollying people along. I expect you think that people *should* be lively from the minute they open their eyes and that, if they are not, there is something wrong with them. Or perhaps your insufferable cheerfulness first thing in the morning is your way of pumping yourself up so that you can face the day ahead? In this case, I suggest you tiptoe to the bathroom and do your self-affirmations in private in front of a mirror!

Your behaviour leads me to suspect that you are making two basic errors of judgement.

The first one is to assume that enthusiastic behaviour is 'right' and that quieter, less demonstrative people are in some way wanting, or inadequate. This is unnecessarily judgmental and must mean that, on average, you are critical of at least 50% of the people you meet! Extraverted managers often make the mistake of undervaluing quieter, more introverted people. However, with gentle encouragement (accent on gentle!) they have a great deal to offer. They are, for example, good at mulling things over and coming up with carefully considered ideas.

Your second mistake is to assume that leadership is being noisy and leading-from-the-front. Sometimes it *is* necessary to jolly people along, but for most of the time leading is being supportive and leading-from-behind. Charismatic, boisterous leaders tend to attract the headlines and give a distorted impression of leadership. Most leaders are people who are quietly determined and appreciate that they depend on other people if they are to achieve their goals. They understand that leadership is all about creating the conditions where people can flourish and be successful.

So, temper your over-the-top bouts of cheerfulness. Being positive and supportive will suffice.

36

A manager who was punished for exposing dishonesty

Colin was a middle manager in a large utilities company. He headed the job evaluation department and administered the company's job grading system. This involved interviewing job-holders throughout the organisation, composing job descriptions using an agreed format (every job description ended with the words '... and other duties as required'), and scoring the job to establish which of seven salary bands should apply. Colin's department was part of the personnel function and he reported to the Personnel Director.

Colin was an upright, straightforward sort of chap. This was just as well, since he was often offered inducements by those who were keen to 'influence' the job grading system. Senior managers, for example, would lobby him in an attempt to secure a high grade for a newly created job so that it would be easier to recruit high calibre candidates. Colin always managed to resist such pressure and to steer a straight course. He maintained that it wasn't enough to be fair and honest, you had to be *seen* to be. Transparency was essential, otherwise the job evaluation system would quickly fall into disrepute.

The office immediately next door was occupied by Ray, the manager in charge of recruitment and selection. Unlike Colin, Ray was eminently persuadable. In response to requests from senior managers Ray would cheerfully 'adjust his priorities' and let people jump the queue. He accepted small bribes from the recruitment agencies he dealt with – the occasional bottle of whisky or claret and, once, a handsome carriage clock.

Ray also tended to be what he called economical with the truth. You and I would call it dishonest. He would manipulate figures to make it look as if his department was meeting its key targets. He would alter the results of certain psychological tests to improve a candidate's chances of selection. He invented plausible-sounding statistics, conjuring them out of the air precise to the second decimal place.

Each month Colin and Ray would countersign each other's expense claim before it was submitted to the Personnel Director for final approval. Colin was always scrupulously honest with his expenses. He saved all the relevant receipts and completed the form accurately. Ray, by contrast, indulged in some shady practices. He'd claim mileage allowance for journeys he hadn't undertaken and would slip in some receipts that weren't actually work-related. He'd fabricate taxi journeys and attach faked receipts to his claim form.

Aware of these malpractices, Colin felt increasingly uneasy about countersigning Ray's expenses. After a few months, he broached the subject with Ray, who simply laughed, saying life was too short to worry about such trifles. He even offered Colin some faked taxi receipts for his own use. Over the space of a few months, Colin's resentment at being expected to condone Ray's dishonesty festered and grew. Eventually, Colin decided that enough was enough. The next month he would refuse to countersign Ray's form. Colin braced himself for an ugly confrontation, but Ray simply smirked, shrugged his shoulders and said he'd find someone else to sign.

Meanwhile, despite Colin registering his extreme disapproval on a number of occasions, Ray's dishonesty continued. Colin grew more and more troubled by the moral dilemma: Should he turn a blind eye or expose the fraud? One day Ray was boasting about some figures he'd falsified and Colin decided that his silence amounted to cowardly collusion. Come what may, he would have to report Ray's crooked practices.

Colin compiled a dossier and made an appointment to see the personnel director. The director heard Colin out, tut-tutting occasionally and looking suitably concerned. He took the dossier and thanked Colin very much for appraising him of the situation.

Then ... nothing. Life carried on exactly as before. Ray didn't storm into his office and accuse him of being a sneak. Nothing. The only change, and it was so subtle that it took some time for Colin to recognise it, was that the Personnel Director seemed more hostile towards him! He started to find fault with Colin's work and to harry him in a way that hadn't happened before. Then, when the time came for Colin's appraisal, he was criticised for missing deadlines and for general tardiness.

Ray, meanwhile, sailed on unmolested and achieved a good appraisal.

Advice to Colin

Oh dear, you are almost certainly being victimised – paying the price for sticking your neck out and exposing your colleague's fraudulent expense claims. Sadly, in this unfair world, things rarely turn out well for whistle blowers.

Given that you weren't prepared to stand by and do nothing, what could you have done differently to:

1. put a stop to fraudulent expense claims;

2. protect yourself against victimisation?

I realise that I am posing this question after the event, but looking back could help to identify some useful lessons to carry forward. We need to search for things you could have done that might (it is only a might I'm afraid) have led to a happier outcome.

Firstly, I wonder if you could have been more resolute from the word go? Unfortunately you took a few months to work up a proper head of steam. You went through three stages. Initially, despite your misgivings, you colluded with Ray by countersigning his expense claims. Then you reached a stage where you confronted Ray and withdrew your support. Finally, you escalated the whole issue by going to the personnel director. With the benefit of hindsight, I'm sure you can see that the months that elapsed as you progressed through these stages, weakened your case. If only you had made a stand and refused to sign off Ray's expenses when he first approached you, or as soon as you knew that he was being dishonest.

Secondly, you could have campaigned for a change *to the system* rather than singling out Ray as a transgressor. This would have shifted the focus onto how to tighten up the processes that 'allowed' fiddling to take place. It is likely that other people, not just Ray, were taking advantage of loopholes in the system. Your proposals could have saved the company a considerable sum of money without pointing the finger at specific individuals and risking a personal vendetta. Processes don't take their revenge in the same way that aggrieved people do.

Thirdly, you could have canvassed support from a group of sympathisers rather than going it alone. This, of course, assumes that you could have sought out some like-minded people who were prepared to make a stand against wrongdoing. An email, naming no names, might well have done the trick. There is safety in numbers and a co-ordinated campaign would have carried more clout.

Perhaps, even now, you have nothing to lose by campaigning for a more transparent culture in your workplace where people can speak up without fear of reprisals. You could press for a whistle blower's charter that removes the stigmatism associated with being open and honest and builds in safeguards to protect people who are ethical and courageous enough to state their concerns.

37

A manager who thought he was accident prone

Pete was the health and safety manager at a manufacturing company. There were some highly dangerous processes undertaken in the factories in his care and Pete took his job very seriously. It was a high-profile job too because there had been a history of avoidable accidents, even fatalities, in the past and the board had made safety a priority. There were stringent targets for reducing accident rates, and statistics about accidents and near misses were displayed prominently in each factory. There was an elaborate health and safety infrastructure involving trade unions, safety committees, quality circles, monthly reports to the board, a system for sharing best practices, and so on.

On the face of it Pete was a round peg in a round hole – ideally suited to his role. A mechanical engineer by training, he was a rather earnest fellow who tended to take life seriously. He was keen on measurement and loved analysing data and producing graphs and pie charts (much in evidence in all the factories). He was also expert at drafting unambiguous rules and guidelines and was a great believer in making good practices compulsory rather than voluntary. He often said, 'People do what's checked, not what you'd expect.'

There was, however, a strange irony about Pete in his role as a champion for safety; he was accident-prone! Mishaps and accidents seemed to find their way to him in the same way that a moth is attracted to a bright light.

He would happily joke about having more than his fair share of accidents. When he had scrapes in his car, typically he would run into the back of a police patrol car. When he flew in an aircraft there would often be an unexpected technical hitch. Once an engine caught fire one hour out from Heathrow and fuel had to be jettisoned before the plane could return to the airport with numerous fire engines in attendance. When he gave a presentation, the laptop would become disobedient and the table upon which he sat (to give an impression of nonchalance) would collapse without warning. When he cut his hedge, the ladder would slip and he'd need stitches in the hand that had inadvertently touched the blades of his electric hedge trimmer. He actually fell off his roof once while clearing leaves from the guttering and broke his leg in three places.

He also had a track record for, not accidents as such, but absurd mishaps in hotels (the factories he had to visit were all over the country and this often necessitated overnight stays). He was a guest staying at a hotel when the reception area was demolished by a runaway lorry. Another hotel was flooded when torrential rain caused a stream to divert through the dining room. Yet another was attacked by thieves who put all the expensive cars in the hotel car park up on breeze-blocks and made off with the alloy wheels.

Once Pete got up in the night for a pee, and mistook the door to his room for the door to the toilet. It closed behind him and left him standing stark naked in the corridor with the key inside (he was eventually rescued by an astonished night porter). On another occasion he was dozing in the bath when a large middle-aged woman accosted him, insisting he was in *her* bath.

One day Pete paid a visit to a newly acquired factory to chair a safety meeting with the top management team. He hadn't been to this particular factory before and was keen to make a good impression and to put safety issues firmly on the conscious agenda. The meeting was held in a plush boardroom that harked back to Victorian days when the factory had been owned by a wealthy family. Before the meeting Pete had used the management toilet a few doors along the corridor – a splendid place with a stained glass window, a magnificent water closet with a large wooden seat complete with the original brass hinges, and decorative Edwardian tiles from floor to ceiling. Pete subscribed to the Duke of Wellington's dictum that wise men pee when they can and fools when they must. This was an opportunist 'can' pee rather than a 'must' pee and, as Pete rinsed his hands in the generous wash-basin, he relished the finer points of his surroundings.

After a successful but protracted meeting, during which coffee and water had been plentiful, Pete needed a 'must' pee. As he walked down the corridor with the general manager of the factory and other members of the top team, he asked to be excused and dived through the door to his left only to find himself in a cupboard full of brooms, mops, buckets and vacuum cleaners.

Realising his mistake, Pete, paused momentarily to reflect on his predicament. Would it be more dignified to emerge from the cupboard immediately or might it be best to linger, hoping that his colleagues would have walked on and not noticed that he had rushed into a cupboard instead of the toilet next door? He decided that the former would be marginally less damaging to his reputation and reached for the door-handle (a heavily patterned brass original) which turned aimlessly without opening the door. He tried again, but it was clear that the spindle inside the handle had become disconnected.

While he was wondering what to do next, the door opened from the outside. The entire management team was standing in the corridor doubled up with laughter.

Advice to Pete

You may well be joking about being accident-prone, but it is possible that many of your misadventures happen because you *expect* them to. Once you start labelling yourself as an accident-prone person, it makes it more likely that you will be! In some mysterious way, a self-fulfilling prophesy cuts in. Fortunately, research shows that it is unlikely that there is such a thing as an accident-prone personality; just people of different shapes and sizes who seem to attract more than their fair share of accidents.

I think it is important to acknowledge that some of the things that happen to you are due to circumstances completely beyond your control. You are entirely innocent – you just happen to be there, in the wrong place, when lightening strikes. Inevitably, some situations are more hazardous than others – travelling and staying in hotels clearly being just two examples!

When these coincidental mishaps occur, I can understand how easy it is to start to believe that it is either your fault or their fault – 'they are out to get me!' – and to subscribe to some sort of conspiracy theory. But the chances are that 'they' do not exist and that the mishaps belong more to the situation you were in, than to you.

By contrast, it seems likely that some of your other mishaps will not have occurred through happenstance. Your actions will have played a significant part, even though this may not be immediately obvious to you. For example, your haste was probably a contributory factor when you finished up in a broom cupboard instead of the toilet. Ladders that slip and falling off roofs are clear examples of accidents brought about by a number of factors – you being one of them.

But, as a heath and safety manager, you'll already appreciate that accidents are usually multifaceted – brought about by a mixture of interrelated factors that are difficult to unravel and isolate.

In practice, there are two basic ways to reduce your exposure to accidents. Firstly, you could identify accident-prone *situations* and plan to avoid them. This would reduce the coincidental mishaps. Secondly, dare I suggest that you could be more safety-conscious! You could significantly cut your accident rate by preparing better and taking more care on those occasions when your actions are a contributory factor.

Whatever you do, cast aside any assumptions that you are an accident-prone person. Avoidance and prevention – those are the two routes to a long, accident-free life.

38

A manager who prided himself on his time management

Richard was an ambitious middle manager in an insurance company. He used every opportunity that came his way to impress anyone who might increase his chances of promotion. Impeccable time management was one of his many attributes. He took great pride in his timekeeping and had built up an enviable reputation for punctuality. Years previously he had attended a time management course and become entranced by the procedures and techniques it advocated.

The discovery that things were either urgent or important, but rarely both, was an astounding 'aha' moment for him. Similarly, the realisation that everything he did fell into one of just two categories – reactive or proactive – was, for Richard, little short of a Road to Damascus experience!

As you might expect, Richard was a keen advocate of the diary system that had been an integral part of the course he attended. He could hardly move without a prioritised To Do list prepared the day before. He guarded his discretionary time as if it were the crown jewels. Richard insisted on 'batching' interruptions into two consolidated 30-minute periods, one in the morning and one in the afternoon. He hung a notice on his office door so that people knew whether he was interruptible or not! Whenever someone inflicted an unscheduled interruption on him, he would leap to his feet and remain standing throughout because he had read about a piece of research that proved that this would reduce the length of the interruption.

Richard's team meetings (he called them 'huddles') were also conducted at a brisk pace, with everyone standing, and with a timer on the table set to ring at the planned finishing time. If you invited him to a meeting, he would insist on being provided in advance with an objective, an agenda and a finishing time. If these were not forthcoming, he would refuse to attend (unless the meeting was with senior management when, for career advancement reasons, he'd temporarily relax his demands). Generally speaking Richard's high standards were successful in cutting out potentially unproductive meetings.

He only accessed his emails at precisely 16:00 each day and gave himself a maximum of one hour to process them all. His paperwork was ruthlessly divided into three piles; for action, for information and for reading. Any item that didn't fall into one of these categories was discarded. Needless to say, Richard operated a clean desk policy.

For Richard, using time effectively had become an obsession.

One day, Richard was late for an important meeting with some clients who knew him well. Knowing Richard was a stickler for punctuality, they worried that Richard might have met with an accident. They imagined him unconscious in intensive care, unable to move or send a message to them. Or perhaps he had been abducted, blindfolded and bundled into the boot of a waiting car and spirited away to some remote location? Or possibly he was suffering from amnesia and no longer knew who he was or where he was supposed to be?

With their imaginations running riot, Richard walked into the room.

'Sorry', he said, 'I had a problem with my car.'

'Oh Lord! What was the trouble?' (They conjured up pictures of a high-speed puncture with two complete somersaults, a seized up engine, spontaneous combustion!)

'It was nothing really, I just got into it too late.'

Advice to Richard

Good joke! It certainly sounds as if you've got time management buttoned up. I do wonder, however, whether the techniques you are using have become your master rather than your servant. It all sounds a bit obsessive.

I'm sure you are aware that it is possible to force-fit techniques onto situations and in so doing blind yourself to other possibilities. You may be missing out on the advantages that spontaneity and 'going with the flow' can offer. Haven't you discovered how a promising idea will pop into your head when you aren't trying and least expect it? Or how a solution to a problem will reveal itself while you're walking the dog?

I'm concerned that your strict adherence to time management techniques may be squeezing out time to free-wheel, to toy with possibilities, to play with ideas, to mull things over without the pressure of a time limit or a deadline.

Perhaps you could start by having one day a week (or, if this seems a bit rash, one day each fortnight) that is deliberately time-management free. On this day you would be entirely in reactive mode. There would be no To Do list, no pre-planned 'huddles', no agenda at all in fact. You would just react to whatever cropped up and let events and whims dictate your actions.

After each unstructured, 'rambling' day, write a diary note capturing what it felt like and what you achieved. Experiment with this for at least three months and then review the pros and cons before deciding whether to continue. My guess is that you will find it liberating and that your creativity will be enhanced.

One thing is for sure; you will become clearer when it is advantageous to structure things and when it is advantageous to go with the flow. There is a time and place for everything.

39

A manager who liked to slip away unnoticed

Trevor was an in-company training manager. He frequently ran programmes for young, up-and-coming managers on interpersonal skills. The course, called simply *People Skills*, was a residential 5-day event run in a hotel in deepest Sussex. The hotel stood on a hill in the countryside about 6 miles outside the nearest town.

Trevor was a typical trainer of many years' experience. He had a well-earned reputation for quick-witted banter and amusing small-talk perfected over many years of enforced cheerfulness over countless hotel breakfasts, lunches and dinners. When he wasn't required to perform, he relished periods of solitude when he could temporarily escape the limelight. He would often slip out for short walks when the course participants were safely preoccupied in syndicate groups. There was a churchyard nearby where Trevor would read the gravestones and ponder his own mortality. In these brief periods of reflection, Trevor frequently felt overwhelmed by the futility of running courses, doubting that, in the scheme of things, his life's work was making an iota of difference to anything.

Trevor was always careful to return in good time from these brief respites to visit the syndicate groups and remind them when the next plenary session was scheduled to begin. No one could have guessed that he had been absent and, with his cheerful behaviour back in evidence, no one could ever have imagined that he harboured feelings of self-doubt.

One day, towards the end of a successful week with a particularly responsive group of young managers, Trevor decided to nip into town and draw some money out of the hole-in-the-wall at the local bank. It was Thursday and he knew he'd need some cash to fund the traditional night out at a nearby bowling alley. As usual, the course participants were safely at work in their respective syndicate rooms. Trevor was confident that he would not be missed for the 20 minutes or so that the round trip would take. He jumped into his car and drove the six miles into town. He arrived at the bank and decided to risk parking on double yellow lines right outside the cash-dispensing machine. He put his debit card in the appropriate slot and entered his PIN number only for the display to tell him that the machine was temporarily out of order.

Having retrieved his card, Trevor, still wanting cash, went inside the bank and joined a small queue. He anxiously checked his watch. Exactly 30 minutes before he needed to be back masterminding the plenary. Ample time to return to the hotel as if he had never been away.

Suddenly two men burst into the bank wearing balaclavas and waving shotguns. One gun was trained on the cashier, the other on Trevor and his companions in the queue. The man shouted at them to lie face down on the floor.

The raid was over remarkably quickly and the two men fled with whatever money the cashier had given them. No sooner had Trevor stood up and brushed himself down than the police arrived. No one was allowed to leave until statements had been taken.

Eventually, after two hours, Trevor staggered out of the bank – to find that his car had been clamped!

When at last he arrived back at the hotel after his series of unexpected mishaps, the police were there (a different squad!) talking with the course participants. It transpired that in his absence they had taken a number of impressive initiatives. In the following order they had:

• Made sure that he wasn't asleep in his room.

• Established that he wasn't dallying with the hotel manageress (an attractive lady whom Trevor had remarked on admiringly during the week).

• Phoned his office and his home to find out whether he had left any messages with them.

• Discovered that his car was missing from the hotel car park.

• Searched the lanes in the immediate vicinity of the hotel to check that he wasn't slumped over the steering wheel having suffered a heart attack.

• Reported him missing to the local police.

The experience cured Trevor's tendency to slope off during syndicate exercises.

Advice to Trevor

If you have been cured of wandering off during break-out sessions, you will need something worthwhile to occupy yourself.

I can quite understand that you want the syndicate groups to be self-sufficient and that you have no ambitions to become an interventionist. I think this is admirable – in my experience far too many trainers feel compelled to rush around visiting the groups and intervening needlessly. This is either because of an inability to let go or because they feel guilty if, having set everyone else to work, they have nothing to do!

So, what are you going to do during these breaks? You could of course read a book or do a crossword – but I suspect this will not satisfy you for long and that soon you'd be nipping out on one of those morbid visits to the local churchyard!

What you need is an activity that:

- uses the syndicate groups as an invaluable resource;

- keeps you gainfully occupied so that you are not tempted to start intervening for the sake of it;

- focuses your attention on the dynamics of the groups, not the content of their deliberations.

My recommendation is that you become an expert in behaviour analysis. Studying the interactions between group members is endlessly fascinating – but only if you get into the detail of what people are saying and their body language.

You could start with a simple category system where you check off how often people seek ideas, suggest ideas and the various reactions to them. You could work out the ratio of positive reactions to negative reactions and even break this down into building/supporting and disagreeing/difficulty stating. You could monitor the number of questions asked and contrast this with the number of statements made. You could study eye contact, hand gestures, who is talking to whom, the number of times people nod their heads to signify agreement, what people's feet are up to under the table. You could concentrate on the leadership behaviours of the chairperson or the person with the flip chart.

There is literally no end of stuff like this to study — and you have a ready made laboratory right there each time you run a programme with small group activities. You could form new hypotheses to test, and publish your discoveries. In no time at all you would get a reputation as an authority on group dynamics and be invited to present papers at international conferences. Occasionally, you could even feedback some of your findings to the course members — but this would be a spin-off rather than the main purpose which is to keep you gainfully occupied.

40

A manager who oozed clichés

Clive was the marketing manager of a large travel agency. In his mid-40s, with three children and a mortgage, Clive was an unremarkable but perfectly sound performer. He prided himself on being an original thinker, and was a menace when working with marketing agencies because he used to feel obliged to produce the last idea and was forever changing his mind, usually after a critical deadline had just passed.

Clive worked at the company's headquarters alongside other managers all heading up central functions. Clive hadn't always been in the travel business, having held a variety of jobs in different sectors. However, marketing had been his passion from college days onwards. If there is a stereotype of a marketing man, Clive was it. He radiated faith along the lines of 'it's not the sausage we sell, it's the sizzle'.

Now, as you might guess from the mention of sausages and sizzle, Clive was very fond of catch-phrases and clichés. He frequently made remarks such as:

'Let's get to where the rubber hits the road.'

'That's about as useful as tits on a bull.'

'No rest for the wicked.'

'What you lose on the swings, you gain on the roundabouts.'

'His bark is worse than his bite.'

'We're stuck between a rock and a hard place.'

'It's all water under the bridge.'

'The road to hell is paved with good intentions.'

'We're on a hiding to nothing.'

'There's more than one way to skin a cat.'

And so on. Clive appeared to be oblivious of his addiction to cliché-speak. Even when people made fun of him by mimicking his clichés, Clive didn't seem to notice. One had to conclude that it was all happening at some deep, unconscious level.

In addition to using clichés on a daily basis, Clive would also develop a fondness for a particular catch-phrase that would last for two or three weeks before fading away to be replaced by another. For example, at a time when Clive had 'discovered' systems thinking, he drove his colleagues to distraction by frequently uttering meaningfully, 'It beats as it sweeps as it cleans.' While it lasted, it was extraordinary how many things Clive perceived as total inter-linked integrated systems.

Another example was when Clive realised that there were few absolutes and that just about everything was relative and open to differing interpretations. While in the grip of this not insignificant insight, Clive used to go round saying 'There's no perception without contrast.' Yet another example was when Clive returned from holiday with a T-shirt displaying on the front, 'When all is said and done …' and on the back, '… far more is said than done.' For many weeks Clive used to say this as he emerged from yet another management meeting.

One day Clive was serving on a selection panel charged with the task of recruiting an advertising manager. Naturally, creativity featured high on the list of competencies in the person specification and the panel was at pains to assess this attribute with each of the five short-listed candidates.

During the review session at the end of the day, Clive opened the proceedings by saying 'We are here to sort the wheat from the chaff – but I fear all we have is chaff.' His colleagues asked him to be more explicit and were astonished to hear him express the view that all the candidates had been 'too ordinary'.

When challenged to substantiate this claim, Clive said he'd failed to detect sufficient original thinking and, in particular, had been disappointed by the number of hackneyed phrases they had all employed!

Advice to Clive

You seem oblivious to the absurdity of rejecting candidates because they do exactly what you do. This is an interesting reversal of the usual problem of selecting people in your own likeness!

Your tendency to speak in clichés, besides driving your colleagues mad, suggests a lack of originality. Since you pride yourself on being an original thinker, no doubt you will dismiss being cliché ridden as a harmless foible – an irrelevance in the scheme of things. But your habit of speaking in clichés cannot be doing your reputation much good. You appear to be oblivious that you are doing it and blissfully unaware that your colleagues are quietly taking the mickey.

Somehow you need to be alerted to the number of times you repeat a cliché or a catch-phrase. Have you got a close colleague who could monitor your clichés when, say, you are in meetings together? All they would need to do is jot down the clichés you use and then 'score' the number of times you utter each of them using a simple tally-mark system. If they also note the elapsed time, you would even be able to work out the average number of clichés used per hour.

Hopefully, this sort of monitoring would make you sufficiently self-conscious that you would soon be able to catch yourself employing a cliché. Once aware of the tendency, the next stage would be to train yourself to nip the cliché in the bud (if you will forgive the cliché!).

Clearly, this isn't a life-threatening problem. But it is harming your reputation, and it is surely a relatively easy habit to eradicate. Improvements to performance (and reputation!) are often achieved by making small adjustments to behaviour. It is surprising how the little things count.

41

A manager who encountered fierce resistance

Daniel was a senior scientist who had taken early retirement from an agricultural research establishment. He had had a distinguished career, publishing many academic papers and had led a team with an international reputation. Besides being a successful scientist, he also prided himself on his business acumen having worked all his career in the commercial sector.

Daniel was tall, bearded and well-meaning. After a few months of retirement, when he had redecorated the house inside and out and conquered the garden, he looked for something else to do. His wife, though fond of him, was also keen for him to find an outside interest. For many years she had been used to having the run of the house during normal working hours without anyone getting under her feet. She ran a small PR agency from an office at home and she was finding it hard to adjust to having a husband at a loose end.

In his spare time, one of Daniel's near neighbours was chairman of the local marriage guidance council. Over the past couple of years when they met at social events, they had had a few conversations about marriage guidance and Daniel knew that his neighbour was casting around for a successor. After some thought, Daniel volunteered to become involved and was invited to one of the committee meetings.

Daniel was welcomed with open arms as someone with useful

business experience and with time on his hands. At the next AGM, Daniel was proposed and seconded as the next chairman and voted in unopposed. The retiring chairman couldn't disguise his relief.

Daniel took to his new responsibilities with typical thoroughness and set to work to tackle some of the problems that faced the charity. His predecessor had briefed him on these and identified the key problems.

There were three priorities. Firstly, to improve the finances. Apart from voluntary donations, they were totally dependent on grants from the local authority. Secondly, to find some way to reduce the embarrassingly long waiting list of clients asking for an appointment. Daniel knew that marriage guidance councils were not set up to provide an emergency service, but he considered that having to wait six weeks or more for a first appointment was unacceptable. Thirdly, to find out why there was such a disparity between the 'productivity' of different counsellors. The figures showed that, on average, some counsellors would have three or four one-hour sessions with each client, while others would have twelve to fifteen sessions. Daniel was very puzzled by these differences.

Daniel soon found that whatever he suggested was met with fierce resistance. Admittedly it didn't help that he kept saying, 'When I was in business we used to ... .' There were many instances where Daniel's ideas from the commercial world triggered outrage. For example, he suggested that they should introduce a minimum charge for counselling sessions and encourage those who could afford it to pay more. This was howled down by the counsellors, who insisted that the service had always been accessible to all, irrespective of their ability to pay. He suggested that they should try to raise funds from new sources – perhaps from employers in the area, arguing that marriage guidance reduced stress and absenteeism. But the majority of counsellors were strongly of the opinion that it was right and proper that the local authority should continue to provide the funding. He suggested that the waiting list could be cut by having some counsellors who saw clients promptly to make an early assessment of their needs and decide whether they should be allowed to jump the queue. Shock, horror – this would create a dangerous precedent and mislead people into thinking they were an emergency service like the Samaritans.

Within a few weeks, poor Daniel was feeling that he was in an impossible position. He had never before come across a group of people who were so risk-averse, so determined to resist change. At work there had, of course, been many instances of resistance but somehow it had been easier to win over hearts and minds and, as a last resort, to impose a change. With volunteers it was a totally different experience. There was no way to insist on a change without risking them going off in a huff and the whole service collapsing.

Meanwhile, the waiting list grew longer. In desperation, Daniel called a special meeting of the counsellors where he gently, ever so gently, suggested that the counsellors with a typically fast turnover of clients could compare their working practices with those who tended to take longer to achieve, ostensibly, the same outcome. He hoped that some good practices might emerge that would help to improve overall productivity.

Unfortunately, none of the counsellors took to the notion of 'productivity' and some, inevitably the ones who tended to have numerous sessions with the same client, immediately took offence. This was no less than an attack on their professionalism, indeed on their integrity. Did he for one moment imagine they were hanging onto clients for longer than was absolutely necessary? The idea was outrageous! They, and they alone, were trained to judge when their clients were ready to disengage from the counselling process.

Doing his best to appear undaunted, Daniel cited some figures showing that the national average was six counselling sessions per client and that some of the counsellors were greatly in excess of this. This, of course, was a terrible mistake! It was naïve of him to imagine for a moment that statistics, from whatever source, would win the day. He was met by a barrage of objections – the need to be client-centred, how averages were misleading, how statistics proved nothing, how each client's needs were unique … and so on.

Daniel went home to his wife, a broken man. Like all rational scientists, he licked his wounds and pondered his experiences for a few days before calmly resolving to resign at the next AGM.

Advice to Daniel

Have you reflected on why your ideas stirred up such fierce resistance? Are you inclined to blame the counsellors for being awkward and obstructive? Or, might the ideas themselves have been inappropriate? Or, do you think the ideas were sound and that the problems you encountered were more to do with your influencing style? Or, might it have been a mixture of all of these?

Let's assume it was a mixture (it usually is!).

It was predictable that the counsellors would be touchy and resistant. Volunteers, by their very nature, tend to be passionate about the worthwhileness of their cause and stubbornly independent. They are especially wary of anyone who tries to organise them and to trespass on their freedom to exercise what they regard as their professional judgement.

I also think that, with a little bit of empathy, you could have predicted that your ideas – essentially to increase productivity – would be likely to be regarded as inappropriately hard nosed and 'commercial'. The volunteers would see them as alien – straight from the dirty world of bottom lines and profits.

And now we come to the real issue; the way you set about trying to win over the counsellors to your way of thinking. As you appreciate, it was important to retain the goodwill of the counsellors. Without this, the whole marriage guidance service could grind to a halt and you'd have a far worse situation than you started with.

Unfortunately, you assumed that the counsellors would see things your way, that the sheer logic of your position would win the day. They, however, saw your proposals as an attack on their integrity. This was bound to cause deep resentment and staunch resistance.

What could you have done to avoid this? Two things.

Firstly, you could have raised the problem of long waiting lists and invited the counsellors to work *with* you to find an acceptable solution. This would show proper respect for their experience and expertise.

Secondly, if this failed to produce an acceptable way forward, you could have suggested your idea and invited the counsellors to build on it. There is a subtle, but vital, distinction between a suggestion and a proposal. Suggestions are ideas expressed as a question ('Would it help if we tried so and so?' 'How about trying so and so?') whereas proposals are ideas expressed as statements ('I think we should do so and so,' 'I propose the following solution.'). Suggestions are tentative and tend to invite positive reactions. Proposals are more take-it-or-leave-it and tend to invite objections. Suggestions pull and proposals push.

Research shows (you are a scientist so I'm sure you'll appreciate some factual data!) that people react quite differently to these two ways of offering up an idea. If you suggest an idea, on 53% of occasions people will react either by supporting it or developing it. If, by contrast, you propose an idea, support drops to 25% and on 39% of occasions it will meet with resistance.

I leave you to draw your own conclusions.

42

A manager who stuck to his story

Duncan was a public relations manager in a leading tobacco company. The PR department was large (understandably, given the increasing criticism tobacco producers faced) and he was one of many young men and women competing for promotion. Opportunities for promotion were scarce. It wasn't quite a question of dead men's shoes – but nearly. When there was a vacancy it was because someone had been moved sideways or left (usually poached by a PR agency who had worked on assignments for the company) or took early retirement.

Duncan was an ambitious chap but also a habitual approval-seeker. All through his schooling, undaunted by teasing from his peers, Duncan had gone out of his way to ingratiate himself with his teachers. Years later, the same polished behaviour patterns were still much in evidence. In the presence of anyone more senior or influential, Duncan would launch a cloying charm offensive – bowing and scraping, fetching and carrying, laughing a touch too loudly at their jokes, agreeing with everything they said. Surprisingly, most of his seniors were taken in and found themselves wishing that more young people were as agreeable and compliant.

So, all things considered, the chances of Duncan's achieving a promotion were high. It was just a question of not making a blunder, keeping his nose to the grindstone and using every opportunity that came his way to enhance his reputation with his seniors. Duncan settled down for a long haul and regarded the challenge as a PR exercise in its own right – with himself, rather than tobacco, as the 'product'.

When it came, Duncan's opportunity for promotion was completely unexpected. Duncan's immediate boss was, literally, caught with his pants down, having energetic sexual intercourse with a woman from one of the outside agencies. Apparently, in the grip of an uncontrollable lust, he had failed to lock the door to his office. A director, who happened to be passing, dropped in unannounced to discuss some amendments to a draft press release. He was astonished to find a half-clad woman spread-eagled on the desk with Duncan's boss wedged between her thighs. The cavorting couple were only given time to adjust their clothing before being frog-marched out of the building to oblivion.

After the shock of this sudden turn of events had worn off, Duncan, among many others eager for promotion, put in an application for his disgraced boss's job. The selection process was to be rigorous: a screening interview with an outside agency, some psychometric tests and a final interview before a panel of senior managers. Duncan fully appreciated that this was one of those rare, unplanned moments in life that need to be fully exploited. He made careful preparations for the interview, listing all the questions he was likely to be asked and devising impressive answers. He also worked out what questions he could ask that would distinguish him from the other applicants. He rehearsed, over and over again, the answers he would give to the questions he expected. Not surprisingly, he anticipated that one of these questions would be about his strengths and why he thought he should be offered the job.

He prepared a careful answer that included a long list of his relevant skills and affirmed his belief that customers were king and that the company's reputation was totally dependent on good PR. It also went on to say that tobacco was a wonderful product that relieved stress and brought happiness to millions of people around the globe. It was rousing stuff deserving of a drum roll and a fanfare of trumpets.

Duncan sailed through the first interview. He was pleased to be on the shortlist but disappointed not to have had the opportunity to boast about his skills and make his speech eulogising tobacco.

However, at the final interview before a panel of senior managers, he was asked the question he had predicted and had rehearsed so thoroughly. Duncan drew in his breath, expanded his chest, and delivered his prepared answer like a Shakespearean performer overacting at a crucial audition.

When he had finished, there was a stunned silence. The chairman of the board cleared his throat, gazed unblinkingly into Duncan's eyes, and said, 'Right! I want you to go outside for five minutes and think of the real reason.'

Before leaving the room Duncan managed to splutter some feeble protests, but to no avail.

In the corridor, seized with panic, Duncan wondered what to do to retrieve the situation. Would it be best to stick to his guns and thus win points for consistency – even for holding his nerve under pressure? Or might it be more impressive to change his answer and demonstrate admirable flexibility? An appalling quandary – not helped by the fact that some of his rivals for the job passed along the corridor and asked him cheerfully how it was going.

After five minutes, Duncan went back into the lion's den and repeated his pre-prepared answer with even more forced conviction than the first time.

He wasn't offered the job and his wife berated him for having bungled the chance. Duncan comforted himself by recalling that PR was the art of making whole lies out of half-truths. It was just that he wasn't yet good enough at it.

213

Advice to Duncan

Shame about the interview – particularly since it was a rare example of you sticking to your guns and not ingratiating yourself by falling in with what was expected. Never mind, the important thing now is to address the central problem; your addiction to approval-seeking behaviour.

Numerous past experiences will have reinforced the notion that you should please people in power. As a consequence, seeking approval has become a habitual behaviour pattern; an automatic, knee-jerk reaction whenever you encounter anyone in authority. But you should ask yourself whether you are prepared to spend the rest of your career kowtowing to your seniors.

There are, of course, some advantages. Some bosses will enjoy your deference and you will get a reputation for being an agreeable sort of fellow who is good at maintaining harmonious relationships. This undoubtedly leads to a more comfortable existence, both for yourself and for those around you.

Now weigh these advantages against the disadvantages. You may struggle to identify significant disadvantages so here are some for starters:

- You will be motivated to find the most popular path rather than the one you really think is best.

- You will avoid communicating bad news (fearing that the messenger will be shot!).

- You will be inhibited in conversations with seniors, careful not to put a foot wrong.

- You will tend to make promises that you probably can't fulfil.

- You will give people the impression that you are in total agreement even when you in fact have doubts and reservations.

- You will find it difficult to say no, and find yourself obliged to do things you resent.

- You will get angry with yourself for not being authentic and speaking your mind.

- You will feel dependent – that your destiny is in other people's hands and that they must be pleased with you.

Perhaps, as you ponder the downsides of being an approval seeker, you can add to this list. I hope so because you need to convince yourself that the disadvantages exceed the advantages. Anything less and it is predictable that you will continue to seek the approval of your seniors

It would be a mistake for me to attempt to persuade you to change (you'd probably agree with me for the sake of peace!). It is only by taking responsibility for your own actions that you can free yourself from deference and become your own man.

43

A manager with a low tolerance for ambiguity

Al was a training manager in a multinational company. In a previous existence he had been a chemical engineer.

Al was an extraordinarily well-organised person. His tolerance for ambiguity and uncertainty was abnormally low. This meant that, over the years, he had adopted certain rigid disciplines designed to keep chaos at bay. For example, he always wore the same clothes on fixed days of the week – a blue shirt on Mondays, fawn on Tuesdays, white on Wednesdays and so on. He always drove exactly the same route to work, leaving home at exactly the same time each morning. He always took a one-hour lunch break, between 13:00 and 14:00, during which time he ate sandwiches prepared by his wife and read *The Times*, obituaries first, letters second, leaders third, and finishing off with the quick crossword.

He adhered to identical, well-worn rituals when preparing to run a course (a major part of his job). He had detailed checklists of all the handouts in chronological order of use. Each was two-hole-punched so that course participants could file them in the ring-binders Al prepared for them – each with the correct number of dividers and each with a label on the cover showing the person's name. Visual aids received the same loving care. Take it from me, this man was highly organised!

One of the odd things he used to do when running a course was to blow a shrill blast on a whistle whenever he wanted to command attention – like a scoutmaster or a football referee. In the opening session of each programme he ran, Al would demonstrate the whistle and solemnly explain its significance. It meant, he would tell an incredulous room full of young managers, that when they heard the whistle, they must stop doing whatever they were doing and listen to him!

One of the programmes Al ran from time to time used outdoor activities. At prescribed intervals throughout the course participants had to sit in quiet reflection and write a learning log entry. The learning log invited them to focus on a recent experience, describe what they had learned from it and indicate what they were going to do differently in future. Al explained that this was a mandatory requirement and that two blasts on the whistle would herald a period of reflection and that, after exactly 15 minutes (Al also carried a stopwatch) a single blast would mean that normal life could resume. If during the 15-minute period anyone dared to speak, or do anything other than think and write notes in their logs, then Al would extend the period for reflection by adding on whatever time had already elapsed.

Theoretically, this meant that reflection time, once started, could last for ever. Naturally, no one wanted this to happen, so compliance with the 'no speaking/no doing' rule between blasts on the whistle was understandably high.

Somehow, in the outdoor environment under open skies and surrounded by fields and trees, the whistle came into its own! It didn't seem quite so absurd as it did when inflicted on people within the confines of an ordinary classroom. Course participants could be spread over a hillside, or abseiling down a rock face, or in the middle of assembling a raft from oil barrels, planks and ropes, only to stop in their tracks when they heard the fateful two blasts on Al's whistle.

Conversation would cease, out would come learning log booklets, people would look suitably reflective, chew on their pencils and make the occasional note.

So long as participants were totally compliant during the 15-minute periods, Al was not in the least interested in what was being recorded in the logs. Nor did it ever occur to him to keep any sort of log himself.

Three days into one particular course, a young manager met with an accident and had to be carried off to hospital with a broken leg. Not surprisingly, he left his ring binder of handouts and learning log booklet behind. When his colleagues turned the pages of his log they discovered that he had filled it with entries such as:

'What a waste of time this reflection bit is. I'll just have to look as if I'm doing it until the time limit is up.' And, 'If brains were taxed, this whistle blowing maniac would qualify for a rebate.' And, most tellingly, 'I'd do *anything* to escape from this learning log caper, short of breaking a leg.'

It seems that, on further reflection, he had decided that breaking a leg was a worthwhile sacrifice!

Advice to Al

Oh dear! Being organised is one thing, but your insistence on rigid routines and an orderly existence sounds as if it has taken on a life of its own. It has become compulsive. Your low tolerance for ambiguity must mean that your main preoccupation is to impose order and avoid the anxiety that any sort of disorder triggers. This inevitably turns you into a control freak – not a good characteristic for a manager who has to be flexible in the face of numerous changes and uncertainties.

It will not be easy for you to break the behaviour patterns you have perfected over the years – but it *is* possible and you will feel *much* happier with yourself (and others) if you can pull it off.

The key to success is to appreciate that you are imposing control on a hostile world in order to reduce your feelings of anxiety. If you find it hard to accept that this is the underlying motive, just imagine that you are lost in a foreign country where you don't speak the language, where the customs are quite different and where your whistle is ignored. How would you feel? I don't doubt that the answer is extremely anxious!

There are two big snags with being anxious. First, it is not a nice feeling. It is mixed up with feelings of vulnerability and helplessness – and no one enjoys those. Second, feelings of anxiety hinder your behaviour and prevent you functioning at a level you would be perfectly capable of if only the feeling wasn't getting in the way.

What can you do to break the pattern? Four tips.

1. Keep telling yourself that you are *choosing* to feel anxious. It

may sound odd to talk of choosing something like a feeling, but you will have learned when to feel anxious (not *how* to feel anxious; *when* to feel anxious). You weren't born, for example, feeling anxious about organising or running courses.

2. Feelings are not random, they don't just happen in a vacuum; an external event always triggers them. So, have a go at identifying the triggers for your anxiety. The following might feature on your list:

    *   Deciding what to wear in the morning.
    *   Driving to work.
    *   Taking your lunch break.
    *   Making the preparations for a course.
    *   Running a course with a lot of unruly young managers as participants.
    *   Getting course participants to pause for periods of reflection.

    Now ask yourself, 'If I didn't organise these things, what is the worst that could happen and, if it did, would it really matter?' Asking this question may help you to appreciate that these things are not a matter of life and death – are not things worth getting uptight about.

3. Allow yourself to experiment with some changes to your normal routines. Start with the smaller things that have the lowest risk. For example, try wearing different shirts on different days, vary your route to work, change your newspaper from time to time, vary your lunchtime routine … and so on. Gradually work your way up to things that matter more – such as your preparations for a course. These experiments will help you to discover that changes to your

routines do not bring about a calamity. This in turn will reduce your anxiety.

4. Finally, wean yourself off thoughts that revolve around the words 'should, ought and must'. Replace them with the expression 'I prefer'. So, for example, instead of thinking, 'I *should/ought/must* control this' switch to 'I would *prefer* to control this.' A simple adjustment like this to your thinking will help to remind you that controlling things is a choice, not an imperative.

Good luck!

44

A manager who got budget dumping down to a fine art

Giles was a hospital administrator in a large NHS Trust. A qualified accountant, he had always worked in the public sector, initially in local government, then in social services and now in a vast hospital. He prided himself on running a tightly controlled regime where expenditure was closely monitored. He impressed on his staff, and anyone he ever spoke to about the budgeting process and financial controls, that they were entrusted with spending taxpayers' money and that this was a responsibility that shouldn't be taken lightly. Accordingly, all applications for expenditure submitted by the various departments in the hospital were subjected to especially careful scrutiny. Giles would often return an application, particularly if it was for non-medical items such as office furniture, laptops, or even adhesive tape and paper clips, with a note asking that it be fully justified.

However, when it came to operating his own departmental budget, Giles played by different rules. For the first ten months of the financial year he would be frugal, fretting over trivial items of expenditure and making tiny economies. It was as though he really did believe the old maxim that if you look after the pennies, the pounds will look after themselves. However, in the last two months of the financial year, he would change character and indulge in considerable largesse. His staff would suddenly be encouraged to spend, spend, spend. Then, as soon as the new budget came into effect, Giles would revert to being miserly.

Giles, as you've guessed, had developed budget dumping into a fine art. Not only did he jettison surplus funds with a lavish year-end bonanza, he was also skilful at building what he called 'bunce' into the budget. This was achieved by exaggerating items of expenditure at the time the budget was agreed; not too much, just enough to make it easy to under-spend. The combination of bunce in the budget and Giles' frugal behaviour for ten months, guaranteed a handsome surplus by the year end. Having built up a surplus, it was essential to offload it before the next round of budget setting to avoid cuts.

All went well for the first couple of years of Giles's stewardship. The bunce went undetected and the year-ends were marked with joyous spending binges. But then something happened to upset the equilibrium.

The Trust's finance committee decided to clamp down on expenditure. The situation was grave. The Trust had been overspending and was in danger of running out of funds before the year-end. All unnecessary expenditure was frozen with immediate effect and all budgets were to be reviewed as a matter of urgency.

Unfortunately this was announced, without warning, in the ninth month of the financial year – exactly the time when Giles' budget was showing generous surpluses. As it happened, Giles was one of the first to come under scrutiny. The committee was delighted to discover an unexpected nest-egg and the surplus that Giles had carefully amassed was transferred to a central budget.

In the next round of budget setting, Giles's application for an increase in expenditure was firmly rejected. All the bunce was stripped out of Giles's budget and the game was up.

Advice to Giles

You have a say-do gap. Preaching about acting responsibly with taxpayer's money whilst orchestrating budget dumping bonanzas in your own department is a classic example of saying one thing and doing another.

Now that your creative budgeting practices have been thwarted, you might like to reflect on the consequences of failing to 'walk your talk'. I fear one inevitable consequence is that will lose the trust of your colleagues and the people who work for you.

Trust is in the eye of the beholder – a perception based on the extent to which you do what you say you'll do. Every time there is a disparity, your credibility rating goes down. Cynicism about managers 'never meaning what they say' is already widespread. This is one of the reasons why corporate value statements and codes of conduct are, more often than not, a laughing stock. The fine words only serve to remind people of the gap between rhetoric and reality.

Erosion of trust is a serious matter. Consider some of the consequences of being regarded as untrustworthy:

- Regardless of your assurances, people will doubt that you can deliver.

- People will suspect that you are withholding information and being 'economical with the truth'.

- Working relationships will be damaged.

- In negotiations, people will be wary of reaching agreements with you.

- People will be reluctant to commit themselves and go that extra mile.

- People will be guarded in conversations with you and think twice about talking things over candidly with you.

- You'll get a reputation for being two-faced; saying one thing to one person and something quite different to someone else.

Consequences such as these will inevitably take their toll and hamper your ability to function effectively. As a manager, you are largely dependent on the people who work for you. Your power to influence them depends on whether they can believe what you say. Your vulnerability increases in direct proportion to the erosion of trust.

So I urge you to take the necessary steps to close your say-do gap. Modifying people's perceptions of you will take time and effort. Just keep reminding yourself that even though actions have a reputation for speaking louder than words, what really matters is that your words and actions are synchronised.

45

A manager who recommended ways to improve staff motivation

Phil was the manager of a call centre. The centre occupied two open-plan offices where nearly 100 men and women worked. They were divided into teams of eight huddled together at clusters of work-stations. Each team had a supervisor whose job it was, in addition to making their own quota of calls, to keep up morale and spur staff on to even greater heights.

The environment was frenzied and target-driven. There was a constant hubbub as people spoke, with artificial cheerfulness, into their mouthpieces. The walls were plastered with posters tracking performance against targets. There were targets for the number of calls made and the value of the orders secured. Each week a winning team and runner-up were declared and rewarded with air miles. A staff notice board advertised flats to let or share, items for sale, a dog that was looking for a good home and some kittens too.

Something the notices didn't show, however, was the high turnover of staff and the rising absenteeism and sickness rates. Not a week passed without a number of employees ringing in sick and/or handing in their notice. Informal leaving parties at the pub next door provided a steady and lucrative revenue stream for the landlord! Recruiting and inducting new staff was as constant an activity as painting the Firth of Forth Bridge.

Phil was very keen to improve retention rates. Indeed, his boss at head office had made it clear that this was an absolute priority. Constantly having to replace staff pushed up overheads to the detriment of the all-important bottom line. If the so-called burnout problem could be solved, Phil knew he would considerably enhance his reputation with his superiors. His call centre might even become a case study; a model of how to achieve high productivity *and* high morale, rather than one being achieved at the expense of the other.

So, Phil started to investigate the field of motivation at work.

He quickly discovered Abraham Maslow's hierarchy of needs suggesting that workers were motivated to satisfy needs at different levels. Then he read about the work of Elton Mayo at the Western Electric Hawthorne Works in Chicago in the late 1920s and early 1930s. He was fascinated to read about Mayo's investigations into the effects of fatigue and monotony on productivity. He could immediately see strong parallels with the problems he was wrestling with at the call centre. He chuckled aloud when he discovered that the answer was to keep changing things. He began to work out how he could achieve his own 'Hawthorne Effect' by experimenting with certain variables. He could alter the configuration of the furniture, provide more breaks, shorten working hours, experiment with different chairs, intensify the lighting, paint the walls a different colour, turn the heating down, then turn it up again. The possibilities were endless.

However, his plans were soon confounded when he read about the work of Frederick Herzberg and his descriptions of motivators and hygiene factors. He now saw that the variables he wanted to change would merely be tinkering with 'hygiene' and have no lasting impact. He unhesitatingly accepted Herzberg's theory that there were two

227

separate continuums – one that took people from a neutral state up to being motivated and the other that took people from a neutral state down into dissatisfaction.

Phil suddenly saw the world in a different way. Everything fell into two categories; either they were motivating factors or they were hygiene factors.

Fired up by his new found paradigm, Phil wrote a paper for his boss recommending that the way to improve the morale of call-centre staff was to focus on the motivating factors. The key, he enthused, was to find ways to enrich the work itself. He listed the main challenges.

How to give staff:

- a greater sense of achievement;

- more recognition;

- increased responsibility;

- room for advancement;

- opportunities for development.

He also advised that it would largely be a waste of time to invest much effort in improving the hygiene factors since the effects would only be temporary and, at best, people would be raised to a neutral state where they were neither satisfied nor dissatisfied, i.e. *not* motivated.

Phil's boss read the paper carefully but reached a different conclusion. He decided that, by its very nature, call-centre work left little room for manoeuvre when it came to improving the motivators. The answer was to focus on the so-called hygiene factors and to manipulate them so that employees would become discontented about things it would be relatively easy to fix. Management needed to compile a list of things they wanted people to grumble about, then to go through the motions of heeding the complaints and to score brownie points when the deliberate mistake was put right. The food in the canteen was, he decided, a good place to start.

Phil's boss became utterly convinced that manipulating hygiene factors was the way to go. He told Phil that he was surprised other companies weren't using Herzberg's research in this way. Or perhaps they were, but keeping quiet about it?

Phil, appalled at the unashamed cynicism of his boss, handed in his notice – thereby adding to the attrition rates.

Advice to Phil

You might have stood a better chance of persuading your boss to your way of thinking if you had gathered some evidence. Merely making an intellectual case is always less compelling – especially if it is based on work carried out elsewhere by academics. You needed some proof that focusing on Herzberg's motivating factors raised staff morale and reduced absenteeism and/or attrition in *your* call-centre.

Evidence is hierarchical. The highest form is arrived at scientifically by using multiple randomised controlled trials. As the name implies, this is painstaking stuff, usually carried out over a lengthy period, and requiring some professional expertise. You'll be relieved to hear that I'm not suggesting that it was necessary for you to go this far! Fortunately there are lesser sorts of evidence that are still far more convincing than relying on third-hand claims and theories.

You could, for example, have conducted some straightforward experiments yourself, possibly with just one of the call-centre teams. This would have given you practice, as opposed to scientific, evidence. You could have tried, say, introducing a 10-minute break after every hour and monitored the effect that had on productivity, morale and absenteeism. You could have introduced some stress-busting sessions. You could have involved staff by soliciting their ideas on ways the work and/or the working environment could be improved. The act of consulting the staff, combined with being seen to implement some of the forthcoming suggestions, would undoubtedly have improved morale. But you already know this from reading about the Hawthorne Effect.

At the very least you could have surfed the web and found out about work done in other call-centres to combat low morale and high staff attrition. A search in Google would have produced thousands of potentially useful case studies. This would have given you anecdotal evidence – not as impressive as practice evidence, but better than nothing.

A combination of practice and anecdotal evidence would have strengthened your hand considerably and made it much more likely that you would have won over your boss.

But come to think of it, why did you need to persuade your boss? You were the call centre manager. Surely you were empowered to go ahead and do whatever was necessary to solve the problems and lift performance? If not, then in my view you should still have gone ahead until you were told to stop. It is fascinating how often people don't do something because they *think* they are not allowed to.

And by the way, Herzberg's work does not offer you an 'either-or'. My reading of it is that it is best to pay attention to both hygiene factors *and* motivating factors. Handled properly, the former prevent negative dissatisfaction and the latter promote positive satisfaction.

46
A manager who thought he had overslept

Charles was a senior HR consultant in a firm of international consultants. He led a team who specialised in advising on remuneration and incentive schemes. It was company policy to accept invitations to speak at important conferences and, often, to have an exhibition stand for the duration of the conference. Charles thoroughly enjoyed delivering keynote addresses. He was an accomplished public speaker who loved to amuse audiences with jokes and anecdotes. Unsolicited feedback confirmed that listeners enjoyed his sessions and the whole experience was satisfying to his ego.

However, Charles did not at all enjoy manning the exhibition stand. He didn't relish the inevitable standing idly about and also felt awkward greeting passers-by and trying to cajole them into showing some interest in their services. He regarded addressing a captive audience, with all the advantages of a raised stage, microphone, podium and visual aids at the touch of a button, as a dignified activity. By contrast, touting the company's wares on an exhibition stand felt, well, demeaning – like a prostitute loitering in the doorway of some seedy club. Not that the company stand was in the least seedy – in fact it was quite grand and had won awards at previous exhibitions.

Charles did his best to conceal his discomfort and passed the time in ostensibly cheerful banter with visitors and, when there weren't any of them, with the glamorous women who ran the neighbouring stands.

232

One day Charles received an invitation to deliver a keynote speech at a conference in Malaysia. Unfortunately the date of the conference was not convenient. Two days before it a crucial board meeting had been scheduled at which Charles was due to give a paper outlining the five-year plan for his department. Two days after it Charles was already booked to perform at a conference in San Francisco. So the trip to Kuala Lumpur would have to be a swift 'in and out' affair. Secretly, Charles was pleased about this. It meant he would only have time to give his speech and the distasteful business of hanging around the exhibition stand would be left to others.

As it turned out, at the last minute the board meeting was postponed, but by then it was too late for Charles to alter his travelling arrangements. Then, on the day he was due to fly, there was a security alert at Heathrow and the flight was delayed. Charles sat in the business lounge, sipping whisky and dry gingers, rehearsing his speech.

Once the flight was called, there was a further delay waiting for some passengers to board who were taking longer to pass through immigration than had been expected. Charles calculated that he would reach the hotel in Kuala Lumpur only just in time for the speakers' briefing the evening before the conference opening.

At the briefing, the organisers explained that an important government minister was going to declare the conference open at 09:00 the next morning and that all the speakers needed to be in the hotel foyer at 08:30 sharp to be presented to the minister. Well seasoned in such matters, Charles unpacked his case, put his trousers in the press, ironed the creases out of his shirt, organised a morning call for 07:00 and fell into bed to catch up on some sleep.

He awoke with a start and consulted his wristwatch on the bedside table. He was appalled to see it was already ten minutes to nine. He leapt out of bed, cursing the hotel for failing to call him, and got into the shower without waiting for the water to run hot. As he stood there (the water was tepid by now) it slowly dawned on him that it was still dark outside, and very quiet. Puzzled and disoriented, he got out of the shower and looked at his watch again. This time it said twenty past three.

He realised that when he first consulted his watch it had been upside down. Twenty past three looks exactly like ten to nine if your watch is upside down – especially if it has dots and dashes rather than actual numbers.

After his cold shower, Charles couldn't get back to sleep. He was on parade at 08:30 sharp ready to shake the minister's hand and to be garlanded with orchids. He was amused to see that two of the other overseas speakers had overslept.

Advice to Charles

Either get a watch with a face that you can read at a glance or a digital travelling clock that cannot be stood upside down and has large numbers that glow in the dark!

You might also like to make your globe trotting less manic. How about making it a rule that you will always reach a destination at least 24 hours before you are on duty? 48 hours would be even better. This would give you time to acclimatise and build in some contingency time in case of delays. You might even be able to do some sight-seeing! It seems a shame to visit so many interesting places only to see the airport and the inside of a hotel.

47
A manager who was too big
for his boots

Tim was a young, ambitious middle manager in a large retail outlet. He had joined the store as a graduate management trainee and quickly risen through the ranks to become an assistant departmental manager. He was confident and cocky, spoke with assurance and was always smartly turned out. He was careful to hide his occasional mistakes and had the happy knack of always looking busy – even when he wasn't.

Tim was assistant manager in the carpet department. Previously he had held an equivalent position in the bedding department, but had quickly fallen out of favour with his boss. There seemed to be two interrelated problems. Firstly, Tim tended to be arrogant and to treat his boss with disdain and, secondly, his boss found him inappropriately flippant. He complained that Tim made up for his superficial knowledge of beds, particularly mattresses, by telling customers half-truths and downright lies. Tim's boss was a dour Scot and, not normally demonstrative, he had flown into a rage when he caught Tim bouncing up and down on a bed with a couple who were engaged to be married. Tim claimed it was a brilliant way to test the bed prior to what he imagined would be bouts of energetic love-making. Tim received an official reprimand and was transferred side-ways to the carpet department.

Unfortunately, Tim's new manager, Neil, didn't rate Tim any more highly. Both managers were good friends and they compared notes about Tim's carefree style. Neil had not had the advantage of a university education and was exceedingly envious of Tim's graduate status and very irritated by his misplaced confidence.

Neil would seize every opportunity to cut Tim down to size. But somehow Tim, with his cheerful demeanour and ability to speak persuasively, always managed to emerge unscathed from Neil's spoiling tactics. This, of course, only served to further antagonise Neil.

One day, Tim was serving a customer – a woman in her early seventies who had spent a long time rummaging through piles of small rugs of different qualities. The rugs were sorted into piles depending on the quality and price. Tim had already greeted the customer and asked if he could help, but she had said she was 'just looking' so Tim had withdrawn to allow her to examine the rugs at her leisure.

After waiting a reasonable time, Tim approached the customer again and this time she was ready for his assistance. She had selected a rug that she very much liked but explained that she couldn't pay for it until Thursday when she received her next pension payment. Tim decided to put the rug aside for her and explained that he would put it back in stock if she failed to appear by 17.00 on Thursday.

Thursday came and so did the customer, with exactly the right amount in her handbag. Tim got the rug out to show her again before processing the order. It was only then that he noticed that the label on the back was for £8 more than the customer had been led to believe. Clearly the rug had mistakenly been allocated to the wrong pile. Tim made an instant decision; he would conceal the truth from the customer and let her have the rug for the price she was expecting.

Tim removed the label from the back of the rug and slipped it into his pocket. He made out the invoice for the lesser amount and the customer went off happily. Once she had gone, he tore up the

237

offending label and dropped the pieces in the bin next to his desk. He gave the matter no further thought and went off on his lunch break.

When he returned, he was summoned to Neil's office. The personnel director was there looking grave. On Neil's desk was the label, which had been retrieved from the bin and carefully reassembled with adhesive tape. Beside it was a copy of the invoice Tim had made out for £8 less. An explanation was demanded. Tim told them the full story but, despite his protests, he was dismissed on the spot for cheating the company out of £8.

Neil, and his close colleague in the bedding department, went out for a celebratory drink that evening. They were delighted to have rid themselves of another graduate who, in their view, was a damn sight too big for his boots.

Advice to Tim

It may be harsh, but you have paid the penalty for failing to manage upwards. In a relatively short time, you have succeeded in antagonising two departmental managers to such an extent that they were determined to bring about your downfall. You got your comeuppance.

Treating any boss with disdain is never wise. It is bound to create unhelpful tensions and to make your life more difficult than it would otherwise be. If you have an inadequate boss (none of them is perfect!) it is up to you to extract value from them. In a very real sense, you get the boss you deserve.

Before you get another job, I strongly suggest that you list your expectations of your manager and work out how you are going to shape their behaviour so that it approximates to what you want. The underlying assumption is that behaviour breeds behaviour. In other words, that your behaviour towards them will have an influence on their behaviour towards you. If you look at it this way, it is your behaviour, not theirs, that holds the key.

What sort of expectations might you include on your list? Basically, every member of staff has a right to expect three things from their manager. Everything else you can think of is bound to be a subset of one or more of these.

You need a boss to:

- Clarify your role and responsibilities.

- Give you support and helpful feedback.

- Provide you with ample opportunities to develop your skills and talents.

That's it in a nutshell. Disappointingly, as you have found, very few managers fulfil all three of these obligations and, if any one of them is missing, it is difficult to sustain an excellent performance.

Once you are clear what you want from your boss, you can take all sorts of straightforward initiatives to bring it to pass. If, for example, your role is too vague, you could write your own job description and ask your boss to check it out. If you are lacking feedback on how you are doing, you could ask for some. If you want more developmental opportunities, you could volunteer to tackle some unfamiliar tasks that would stretch you. There are always plenty of things you can do to get added value from your boss.

So, it's up to you to manage your boss. The more effectively you do it, the more your boss's behaviour will improve and any feelings of disdain will evaporate.

48

A manager prone to being caught out

John was a lieutenant in the Royal Artillery on a short-term commission. After a spell in Germany he was posted to Singapore to join the regiment that, in the Second World War, had guns pointing out to sea as Japanese troops entered Singapore in February 1942, having bicycled through the Malaysian jungle.

John was a typical young officer; public-school educated, keen on sport, parties and women. The officer's mess, a fine colonial building set on a hill with splendid views over the parade ground to the blue sea beyond, housed a hard-drinking group of unmarried officers. John frequently drank far more Anchor beer than was good for him (he blamed the humidity!) and ran up some mess bills that stretched his meagre finances to breaking point.

As the most junior subaltern in the officer's mess and the newest arrival, poor John was allocated some of the least popular regimental duties. He was, for example, cinema officer. This wasn't a particularly onerous responsibility. The cinema was run by a sergeant who was in attendance every evening. Each morning the sergeant would arrive with the takings from the evening before. John had to check that the amount tallied with the ticket sales, enter the total in the cinema account ledger, and bank the money. The convenience of having a steady stream of ready cash meant that John sometimes delayed taking it to the bank. Instead he used it to pay off his tailor and fund his carefree lifestyle. Of course, he only 'borrowed' the money and used to make up any deficit by paying in a cheque at the end of the month once he had received his pay.

Once, about half-way through a month, when John owed the cinema account a fair sum of money, the adjutant rang and asked John to report to his office with the ledger and any petty cash he was holding. This was the first time John had been involved in a spot check and he quickly worked out the deficit and rushed round to all his friends explaining the nature of the crisis and borrowing cash. After half an hour or so he had amassed enough petty cash and presented himself at the adjutant's office. He received two rebukes; firstly, for being late and, secondly, for holding too much cash and not banking it frequently enough. Much relieved, John returned the money to his friends and discontinued his practice of borrowing money from the cinema account.

Another of John's unenviable jobs was to look after the regiment's transport. When he first arrived this amounted to a substantial fleet of lorries, gun trailers, Land Rovers and staff cars. However, the regiment was in the process of disbanding and gradually the fleet of vehicles dwindled as they were transferred to other regiments in the area. This wouldn't have been a problem except when senior officers telephoned and demanded transport that John didn't have! Even though he was powerless to solve the problem, various senior officers, expecting an instant taxi service, used to become abusive. As more and more vehicles were disposed of, trying to pacify irate officers over the phone became a daily occurrence.

One day, when all the available vehicles were out on various jobs, the phone rang yet again and, exasperated, John snatched up the receiver and barked, 'Fraser here!' Colonel Fraser was the regiment's

Commanding Officer and at various parties John had amused his colleagues with near-perfect imitations of the CO's voice. The major at the other end of the line apologised profusely, assuming that he had dialled the wrong number. By the time the hapless major had redialled, John, forewarned, had taken the phone off the hook.

John used this trick successfully for some weeks until, out of the blue, the colonel himself telephoned. This had never happened before. On previous occasions when the colonel wanted transport it had always been booked for him by the adjutant's clerk. After John had barked his customary, 'Fraser here!' there was an ominous silence. Then, like an echo, the familiar voice said, 'Fraser *here*! Report to my office at the double.'

The colonel demanded an explanation and John told him about his predicament. Although the colonel seemed sympathetic, even impressed with John's ingenuity, he nonetheless punished him for impersonating a senior officer. John was made duty officer for four consecutive weekends.

The good news was that being gated for a month gave John the opportunity to put his finances on a surer footing.

Advice to John

There is a rather cynical saying along the lines of 'people do what's checked, not what you expect'. Your story illustrates the wisdom of managers doing occasional spot-checks.

You were lucky to get away with the cinema account fiasco. 'Borrowing' money that isn't yours is theft. I'm glad you got a fright. Consider it a wake-up call.

However, don't let the occasional rebuke break your spirit. We need more young managers who are creative and prepared to take risks. You have the makings of an entrepreneur. These are the behaviours I think you should treasure and develop:

- Challenging the *status quo* – everything is *always* capable of improvement.

- Taking responsibility for your actions – especially when things don't go your way.

- Making and taking opportunities.

- Seeing what is important and doing it.

- Taking calculated risks in order to achieve goals you think are important.

- Persevering and remaining cheerful and buoyant in the face of setbacks and difficulties.

- Thinking of creative solutions to problems.

Finally, remember the old adage 'It is easier to ask for forgiveness than for permission.'

49

A manager who reverted to type

Bert was in charge of a large warehouse owned by a mail order company. The picking and packing operation was complex, with a vast number of parcels despatched each day. Thousands of items were stacked in bays on shelves that reached from floor to ceiling. The picking process had recently been computerised but there were still many jobs that required human brains and hands and Bert had some 200 staff, many of them part-timers, to help him.

Bert was an ex regimental sergeant major and still retained many of the behaviour patterns that had stood him in good stead during his 20-year career in the army. He had a ramrod straight back and he didn't walk, he marched briskly. He had steel tips on the heels of his shoes that made loud clicking noises on the concrete floors of the warehouse. In the army he had developed the endearing habit of calling everyone idle. 'Good morning, idle corporal.' 'Good morning, idle guardsman.' This habit he retained as he marched around the warehouse on his morning inspections. 'Good morning, idle packer.' 'Good morning, idle telephonist.' 'Good morning, idle cleaner.' The idle label was applied indiscriminately regardless of how hard people were actually working.

The routine on his morning inspections was also reminiscent of the days when he would inspect barrack rooms or a parade ground full of soldiers standing to attention. In those days he would often fling a soldier's kit out of the window if it wasn't in order. He had also perfected a technique for remembering soldiers on parade from the front *and* the back. One of his favourite tricks was to thrust his hand inside a soldier's belt and if there was any slack to charge the soldier with having 'an idle belt'. Then, having completed the inspection of fifty or more soldiers from the front, he would go down the back of the line, remember the man with the offending belt, repeat the hand test and charge the unfortunate soldier again. Two separate charges for the same idle belt!

Now, back in civilian life, Bert had learned to temper some of these tricks – even though he still marched around the warehouse calling people idle and straightening this and that. Untidiness and litter were pet aversions. He would organise occasional litter parties and sometimes at night he would roam the deserted warehouse picking up rubbish and leaving it on display in the reception area as a reminder that he expected his 'idle' staff to be responsible for tidiness.

A two-day conference was called of all the senior managers. Some months before, the company had been acquired by a bigger German competitor with depots throughout Europe. The management conference was therefore large and multinational. Bert had been invited to give a presentation sharing his experiences during the recent project to computerise the picking operation. Bert prepared his 30-minute presentation with his customary attention to detail. He drafted and redrafted his speech and synchronised the words with PowerPoints showing images of the warehouse. He then learnt the text by heart and rehearsed it until it was perfect.

The conference got underway with an upbeat welcome from the new German managing director. He spoke good English but with a heavy accent. A number of presentations from different parts of the business then followed. Bert's presentation was scheduled to be in the 'graveyard' slot straight after lunch.

During lunch Bert was surprised to find himself feeling uncharacteristically nervous. He picked at his food, excused himself early and went for a swift walk round the conference centre, going over his presentation in his mind. The conference reconvened after lunch and everyone settled down to listen to Bert. His nerves were not helped when a carefully rehearsed John Cleese type joke about not mentioning the war fell worryingly flat. But he pressed on undaunted. About half way through he accidentally pressed the button that brought up the PowerPoints twice which meant that a image upon which he planned to dwell, only appeared subliminally.

Flummoxed by his mistake, and trying to remember how to retrieve the lost visual, Bert reverted to type. He stood to attention, clicked his heels and screeched 'As you were!'

Once a soldier, always a soldier.

Advice to Bert

Your army career has obviously left you with some deeply entrenched behaviour patterns. No doubt many of them continue to be entirely appropriate now that you are running a civilian establishment. However, there are likely to be other habits that you have transferred from the army to the warehouse that are more suspect.

I suggest that you double-check the continued appropriateness of some of your habitual ways of behaving. Check, for example, how people see your tendency to call everyone idle. Some may see it as a harmless, even endearing, characteristic. Others may regard it as an undeserved putdown. Those morning inspections and the litter patrols might also need some adaptation.

As you'll know only too well, the army is a highly structured and hierarchical institution. Successful businesses tend to be less so. The trick is to identify when it is appropriate to employ rigid routines, and demand unquestioning compliance, and when a more relaxed approach would get better results. Both are correct at different times and in different circumstances.

You need to become more pliable and adaptable. The skill is to choose, and use, a management style that fits with the situation. Flexibility is the key.

50

A manager who was prone to tantrums

Geoff was the general manager of a medium-sized supermarket situated on the outskirts of a prosperous town. The store was particularly busy because it had an ample car park, unlike a couple of competitors that occupied premises that were closer to the town centre.

Geoff's store (it wasn't actually *his* since it belonged to a nation-wide group) carried all the usual lines – perishable goods, tins of this and that, wines and spirits, newspapers and magazines. Geoff was slightly overweight and had a decidedly florid complexion (possibly due to overindulging when, for many years, he had been in the wine trade before joining the supermarket as a departmental manager). Unfortunately, he was a man with a low tolerance for mistakes (he called them avoidable human errors). When something fell short of his high standards – and that was often – he was likely to lose his temper. He had reduced many an innocent check-out girl, fresh from school, to tears as he castigated them over some petty inadequacy. His tantrums were, however, short-lived and the more experienced members of his staff had long since learned to sit tight and ride out the storm.

One day, head office phoned Geoff to say that his store was one of three chosen to take part in a customer relations survey. An outside consultant had been hired and would initially spend a day in each store eavesdropping on the interactions between staff and customers. Geoff

249

thought about this and decided not to tell his staff about the consultant's visit because he wanted the store to be seen 'warts and all'.

The day for the visit arrived and Geoff welcomed the consultant and briefed him. The consultant had misgivings about the clandestine nature of the operation and asked Geoff what would happen when staff realised that there was a customer in the store wandering up and down the aisles not buying anything. Geoff told the consultant to refer any members of staff who might have the audacity to challenge him straight to Geoff who would personally deal with the situation.

After an hour or so, the consultant stopped at the vegetable counter to make a note about an exchange he had just heard between a shelf-filler and a distraught customer. Suddenly, a large man pounced on him with a roar and frog-marched him out of the building. The consultant, utterly shocked at being manhandled in this way, managed to splutter, 'Geoff will vouch for me – check with him.'

It transpired that rival supermarkets frequently despatched 'spies' to note prices, particularly of seasonal, perishable goods such as vegetables. The poor consultant, ignorant of this, had unfortunately fished his notebook out of his pocket whilst standing beside the vegetables and been taken for a spy. Geoff, of course, lost his temper with the overzealous 'bouncer' and reinstated the consultant but suggested that it might be safer to make his observations from behind a stack of baked bean tins on special offer – the equivalent of a bird-watcher's hide.

When the consultant had completed his surveys in the three selected stores, a meeting was called to consider next steps in the light of the consultant's preliminary findings. The consultant presented a list of improvement areas he had compiled as a result of his observations. Geoff and the managers from the other two stores were invited to attend, together with some directors from HQ.

As the consultant ran down his list, Geoff held his head in his hands and moaned, 'A can of worms. You've opened a can of worms.' For a while people ignored this odd reaction, but eventually, able to take it no more, a director turned to Geoff and snapped, 'For God's sake shut up, Geoff. We don't stock cans of worms!'

Advice to Geoff

I don't like the sound of your temper tantrums. You are clearly on a short fuse and these sudden outbursts when things don't go your way, can't be good for staff morale or your stress levels.

You probably operate on the assumption that throwing a quick tantrum is an effective way to reduce the occurrence of avoidable human errors (mistakes in anyone else's language!). I expect you also assume that, when you are thwarted by people who do not measure up to your high standards, your anger is a perfectly natural reaction. You'd do well to check the validity of both these assumptions.

Ask yourself just three questions:

1. What evidence do you have that your staff make fewer mistakes as a consequence of being exposed to your temper?

2. Do you think your anger is instinctive or learned?

3. Do you think that your anger is directly triggered by events (i.e. someone making a careless mistake) or that it is *your perception* of the event that does the damage?

The answer to the first question is crucial. You may well find the reverse is true; that people make more mistakes because they are nervous and fearful of incurring your wrath. Alternatively, you may find that your anger makes no difference one way or the other – in which case you are needlessly wasting your energy and risking your health.

The second question goes deeper. If you think your anger is

instinctive, then you are accepting that it is an emotion that cannot be controlled – it 'just happens' to you. If, on the other hand, you believe that your feelings are largely acquired, then this opens up the possibility that you could learn to modify your behaviour; to control your anger, or, better still, actually to prevent it. On reflection, you may decide that your anger is a bit of both; that you learned *when* to feel angry, but not *how* to feel angry. This is a very reasonable point of view and still gives you plenty of room for manoeuvre.

The third question holds the key to preventing your anger. Because your anger is a split second reaction, it is easy to assume that, say, a mistake by a member of your staff is the direct cause. In other words, that the event is to blame. However, if you could accept that the way you *see the event* is doing the damage, then this opens up some exciting possibilities.

Feelings can roughly be divided into two categories; those that help you to function effectively and those that hinder you from functioning as effectively as you might. Generally speaking, anger is a negative feeling that prevents you from taking effective action. You are much more likely to say or do something daft and ill considered under the influence of anger than you are if you were cheerfully calm and collected.

So what's to be done? Overhaul what you are saying to yourself immediately before the anger surges up. Move your thoughts from the left-hand column in the chart overleaf to the right-hand column.

From	To
'They are wrong and I am right.'	'I wouldn't have done it that way myself.'
'They are making a mess of it, I must put them right.'	'They'll soon find out there is a better way.'
'They are doing this deliberately to wind me up.'	'Nothing can *make* me angry. I decide whether or not to get angry.'
'They are incompetent fools!'	'They are inexperienced but doing their best.'
'This is serious/outrageous and ought not to be tolerated.'	'This is disappointing – but nothing more.'
'I can't stand it when things don't meet my high standards.'	'I prefer things to reach my high standards.'

The whole point is to remove the absolutes from your thinking. It is the mismatch between the things you think *should*, *ought* and *must* happen and the things that actually do happen, that triggers your wrath. You can prevent your anger by making your inner thoughts less demanding and more reasonable.

The concept is simple. Putting it into practice is tougher – but, both you and your staff, will be more effective if you can pull it off. You'll live a longer happier life too!

Index

abdication   12, 141
absences, unscheduled   160
accident-prone behaviour   186
accidents   187
acquiescence   164
adaptability   248
advice, guidelines for giving   xii
   seeking   127
anger   252
anxiety, avoidance of   219
approval seeking   211
aptitude tests   32
arrogance   99, 236
assertiveness   44
attitudes, survey of   36
autocratic style   39

band wagons   xxiii, 88
behaviour, analysis   199
   clear signals   28
   development of   244
   impact of   108, 239
   insensitivity   170
   know-all   98
   monitoring   204
   obsessive   194
   patterns   47
   staying calm   42
beliefs   70
Bennis, Warren   xxii
Berne, Eric   132
blame free   71
Block, Peter   xxvi
body language   199
boredom, low threshold   59
brainstorming   145
budget dumping   223
bullying   16, 66, 170
business in the community   79
business plans   60
business schools   19

call centres   226
campaigns   59
'can do' culture   144
carrot and stick approach   160
catch phrases   201
categorising behaviour   23
charisma   58, 89, 180
checking work   150
Citizens' Advice Bureau   19
Cleese, John   247
clichés   201
coaching   5, 96
code of ethics   114
cognitive dissonance   53
command and control   67
communications, authentic   132
competencies   139
confidences, respecting them   118
confrontation   135
consensus   53
consequences, anticipating them   112
   unintended   110
consulting staff   11
continuous improvement   60, 156
control freak   219
Crapper, Thomas   100
crisis management   157
criticism   93
customer relations   249

de Bono, Edward   21
deference   7, 214
delegation   xvi
   phoney   17
Deming, W Edwards   155
democratic management style   54
   when it works best   40
denial   137
dependency   153
developing people   xviii
development suggestions   142

Dictionary, The Oxford English 149
disagreeing 21
discriminatory practices 147
dishonesty 182
diversity 148

eccentricities 107
ego states 132
empathy 170
enthusiasm 58, 176
entrepreneur 21, 89, 109, 244
espoused values 34
evidence, importance of 230
expectations, of a boss 239
    of an employee 83
expenses 182, 222
experiments 90
extra-marital affairs 116

facilitating 135
fad surfing 87
fear in the workplace 156
feedback 37
    360 degree 138
    non-judgemental 136
    solicited 49
    upward 36, 49
feeling vulnerable 172
'finish and go' scheme 109
flexibility 248
Ford Motor Company 73
frustrations, expressed 47
    suppressed 44
future, predicted and preferred 62

games 132
going with the flow 194
Google 231
graduates 16
group dynamics 199
gurus xxiii, 87

habits 245
Harvard Business Review 86
Hawthorne effect 227
health and safety 186
Herzberg, Frederick 227
human resources,
    responsibilities of 131

hygiene factors 227
hyperactive 177

ideas, speculative 21
improvising 60
inertia 163
influencing style 209
initiatives 32, 85, 163
insecurity 172
Institute of Directors 36
interruptions 66
interventions 14

KISS (keep it simple, stupid) 30

lateral thinking 144
leadership course 177
leadership, charismatic 180
    in schools 92
leading xxi
learning from experience 74
learning 217
    logs 74
    formal and informal 76
    sharing with others 77
listening 37
loneliness xx
losing control xvii

management by wandering around 119
management, style 39
    training 104
managers, challenges xvi
    transition to xv
managing, by exception 138
    upwards 239
marriage guidance 205
Maslow, Abraham 227
Mayo, Elton 227
meetings, chairing 46, 52
    guidelines for chairing effectively 56
    rambling 55
    seating positions 94
    skip level 68
mentoring 73, 125
mistakes 249
    deliberate 150
motivation 226

non-directive approach 52
nurturing behaviour 175

Open University 19
Outward Bound 177
overseas travel 233

panaceas 88
people, developing them 97
Peter Principle, The 175
Peters, Tom 119
Pilates 78
planning 59
praise 96
presentations 246
pretence xix
priorities 102
problems 1, 3
  prevention of 155
  solving them 156
  popularity of 157
procrastination 26
production targets 12
profits 85
project work 82
prophesy, self-fulfilling 189

quality assurance 152
questions, asking 121
  open-ended 25, 66, 105
  purposes of asking 27

reflection 217
rehearsals 69
reinforcement, intermittent 102
resistance to change 207
responsibility, getting people
  to take it 152
retirement 205
reviewing 15
rewarding 'bad' behaviour 161
rhetoric 34, 224
role model 116

'say-do' gap 224
selection interview 212
self-awareness 49
self-deprecation 92

self-help books 78
shadowing 74
short-termism 58
should, ought and must 221, 254
silences 64
  tolerating them 65
sitting on the fence 167
social skills 104
speaking up 167
spontaneity 194
staff turnover 17, 226
statistical process control 155
staying in touch 67
strategy 60
successful businesses, criteria for 124
suggesting ideas 210
sycophants 21
systems thinking 202

taking responsibility 215
temper tantrums 249
Thesaurus, Roget's 149
thinking, outside the box 144
time management 191
'to do' lists 191
tolerance for ambiguity 216
training course 196, 217
transactional analysis 131
transparency 185
trust 90, 117, 224
truth, economical with 70
tyrannical behaviour 94

valuing diversity 148, 164
Veblen, Thorstein Bunde 25
victimisation 4, 93, 184
visioning 62
volunteers 209

walking the talk 34, 114, 224
Wellington, Duke of 188
whistle blower 184
win-win 97
winning arguments 98
words, agreeing their meaning 133
work-based learning 74
work experience 79

Endorsements for
50 Cautionary Tales for Managers

From Professor John Adair

Here is a collection of entertaining and instructive parables for managers, written in a clear and readable style. Peter Honey paints the main character in each story with an artist's eye, drawing on his sketchbooks of memories as a management consultant. There are wise lessons here, seasoned with humour, for every manager who aspires to be a good leader of others. An invaluable book.

John Adair
Creator of Action-centred leadership and author of numerous leadership books.

From Sir Christopher Ball

Whether or not you are a manager – and everyone manages something, even if it is only their own time – read this book! It will make you think, make you smile, and make you wiser.

I loved it – and recognise myself in more than one of the stories!

Sir Christopher Ball
Patron, Companion for Learning

From Dr Christopher Brookes

Peter Honey's latest work, *50 Cautionary Tales for Managers*, presents, with all the wit and wisdom that are his trademark, an Elgar-like tapestry of variations on the theme of management and managing – a relationship sometimes overlooked!

Drawing on his extensive experience of facilitating, the author extracts a wealth of insight into those fads and foibles that make managers such an endearing (and at times endangered) species.

Practitioners and students alike will learn much from these tales – frequently chuckling in the process.

Dr Christopher Brookes
Until recently, CEO of the Lifelong Learning Foundation

From Professor Guy Claxton

Packed with Peter Honey's customary wry wisdom, this book holds up a perceptive, occasionally uncomfortable, mirror in which we can recognise our own trademark 'areas for development' as managers – and hopefully be inspired to learn some more!

Guy Claxton
Professor of Learning Sciences, University of Bristol

From Professor Ian Cunningham

Peter Honey has come up with another winner. In his usual clear style he has told simple but valuable stories about real life issues. He is spot on in criticising vacuous lists of desired leadership recipes. Instead, he shows how lively stories can illuminate an array of important problems. The stories are variously funny, sad, depressing, uplifting – but always stimulating. Read and enjoy.

Ian Cunningham
Strategic Developments International

From Anne Evans

Peter Honey is our first 21st century Chaucer; Canterbury Tales becomes Cautionary Tales! You will recognise the characters in this book and they hold our attention throughout. We are all here! There is no avoiding the moral messages of management although each is adorned by clever character masks of the corporate world.

Anne Evans
Chief Executive, HTI

From Sir Antony Jay

Anyone writing a real management book (i.e. for real managers, not for other academics) has a problem; to have universal appeal and relevance the book has to be a general thesis about abstract ideas. But practical, busy managers want entertaining stories about actual managers in recognisable situations.

Peter Honey has solved this problem brilliantly. Drawing on 40 years' experience working with managers, he paints all too credible, and sometimes hilarious, pen portraits of managers we all recognise as authentic. He then uses his deep knowledge as a qualified behavioural psychologist to expose the underlying problem, and propose a solution, in a way that is relevant and helpful to all of us.

Antony Jay
Author of Management and Machiavelli
Co-author of Yes, Minister and Yes, Prime Minister

From Mike Leibling

Perfect! Enjoyable insights and practical ideas for every manager, aspiring manager, and for those who have to work with them!

Mike Leibling
Author of 'How People Tick'

From Dr Bill Lucas

Peter Honey has deservedly gained an international reputation as a learning guru. But this book shows that he is also a brilliant story-teller. 50 Cautionary Tales for Managers is a must read for all managers who are prepared to consider learning how to change their ways for the better (or at least for those who would like to smile at the misfortunes of others who have tried!).

Bill Lucas
Chairman of the Talent Foundation

From Andrew Mayo

Written in Honey's uniquely friendly and down-to-earth style, we are treated to fifty pieces of wisdom woven from real cases of idiosyncrasy, insecurity and dilemma in managers.

Whether a coach, friend or other adviser, here you will find practical and positive ideas – free from jargon and textbook solutions – to give real and empathetic help to those who are blessed with the task of managing others.

Andrew Mayo
Director, Mayo Learning International Limited

From Professor Alan Mumford

The strength of this book is that it personalises instead of generalising about managerial behaviour. Each individual case glows with the heat of a real managerial encounter.

Alan Mumford
Author

From Hugh Murray

A trainer's dream! Enough provocative material to keep people debating almost every management issue you can think of for course after course after course.

Hugh Murray
MD, Scott Bradbury Ltd

From Eric Parsloe

Another Peter Honey 'must read' for anyone seriously interested in helping people understand the role of the manager. Appropriate adjectives fail me but enlightening, entertaining, encouraging, experiential, enthusing, enjoyable, erudite, educative and essential come to mind.

Then again, you could use pragmatic, practical, applied psychology. But I'd advise you to read it and then choose your own.

Eric Parsloe
Founder and MD, Oxford School of Coaching and Mentoring and Oxford Total Learning Group

From Kaye Thorne

Peter Honey is one of the world's leading experts on learning; who amongst us has not had their eyes opened by undertaking his learning styles questionnaire?

In *50 Cautionary Tales for Managers* he shares his experiences of the managers he has met over the last forty years. He candidly describes their characteristics and behaviours and gives wise advice for improvement. Not a traditional management book, this is a valuable resource that can be used for personal development, for managers to use with their teams, or to entertain.

Kaye Thorne
Managing Director of The Inspiration Network